JULIAN OF NORWICH

All shall be well!

William Meninger

JULIAN OF NORWICH

a mystic for today

WILLIAM MENINGER, OCSO

Lindisfarne Books
2010

2010

LINDISFARNE BOOKS

AN IMPRINT OF ANTHROPOSOPHIC PRESS, INC.

610 MAIN STREET

Great Barrington, MA 01230

www.steinerbooks.org

Cover image: *Cloisters*, copyright © by Harley Molesworth
via shutterstock.com
Cover and text design: William Jens Jensen

LIBRARY OF CONGRESS CATALOGING-IN-PUBLICATION DATA

Meninger, William.

Julian of Norwich : a mystic for today / William Meninger.

   p. cm.

Includes bibliographical references.

ISBN-13: 978-1-58420-088-8

ISBN-10: 1-58420-088-X

   1.   Julian, of Norwich, b. 1343. Revelations of divine love.

2. Mysticism. I. Title.

BV4832.3.J863M46 2010

242—dc22

                                              2010024231

Contents

Author's Note

This is a devotional book written to accompany Julian's *Showings*. It is not a substitute for it. To some degree, it is a betrayal of Julian's approach, which is allegorical, non-linear, right-brained, and intuitive. However, for the twenty-first-century mentality, it is probably necessary to introduce some left-brained, systematic thinking. I do this with fear and trembling, hoping that it may facilitate Julian's desire to share her visions with all of her fellow Christians and that it may communicate something of my own love and appreciation for the Lady Julian. The chapters in this book correspond to her chapters as determined by the translation of Edmund Colledge and James Walsh, Paulist Press 1978.

This book is not a translation or a paraphrase of Julian's *Showings* (sometimes called *Revelations*) *of Divine Love*. Rather, it is a commentary intended to provide information, reflections, and some further theological understanding that may serve to enhance the modern Christian's reading of Julian's book. It may be read independently, prior to reading Julian's book, or together with it, chapter by chapter.

INTRODUCTION

Dame Julian of Norwich is alive and well and living in the hearts of twenty-first-century Christians. In his book *Seeds of Destruction*, Thomas Merton, a kindred soul, pays her the ultimate tribute:

> Julian is, without doubt, one of the most wonderful of all Christian voices. She gets greater and greater in my eyes as I grow older, and whereas in the old days I used to be crazy about St. John of the Cross, I would not exchange him now for Julian if you gave me the world and the Indies and all the Spanish mystics rolled up into one bundle. I think Julian of Norwich is, with Newman, the greatest English theologian.

Other than what is contained in her singular work, *Showings*, we know almost nothing of the personal life of Julian. We do, however, know something about her background, as a recluse or anchoress, and the social, cultural, and political life of late-fourteenth-century England.

The fascinating phenomenon of the recluse in England dates from approximately the eleventh century until the Protestant Reformation. During Julian's lifetime there were about forty recluses in and around Norwich, the second largest city in England. They were men and women who were severely screened by the local bishop before they were ceremoniously entombed in their individual cells attached to a local church or religious house. Frequently, they belonged to noble or to wealthy, middle-class, merchant families, as they had to be supplied with the necessities of life and even given the services of one or two servants. Some had been members of a religious or monastic community and were judged to have reached that point, mentioned in the Rule of St. Benedict, where they had profited all that they could from living in community, and were ready to go on to a higher, solitary life somewhat reminiscent of the early desert fathers and mothers. It is possible that Julian had been a nun of a Benedictine house about ten miles from Norwich.

Accepted as holy and wise persons, recluses were often consulted for spiritual direction and sometimes wrote devotional treatises on the spiritual life. We have the testimony of another holy woman from King's Lynn, about forty miles from Norwich, Margery Kempe, who visited Julian in 1413 and found her expert in good counsel during "the many days that they were together." Julian was about seventy years old at the time, having been born in 1342. Records, one from 1416, tell of Julian and her two maids, Sara and Alice, having been bequeathed the sum of twenty shillings. Another will in 1423 also refers to Julian. She probably lived to be eighty years old. Her cell, attached to the eleventh-century church of St. Julian, was destroyed in the Dissolution during the English Reformation, and part of the church was severely damaged by bombs in World War II. It has been rebuilt together with a facsimile of Julian's cell.

ℬ

Although nothing of it is mentioned in her *Showings*, the times in which Julian lived were fraught with political, social, and economic upheavals in both Church and state. There are, indeed, many parallels to the present age. This, in part, helps to explain why Julian speaks so loudly to today after six hundred years of silence.

Julian saw the beginning of the Hundred Years War between England and France, the Babylonian Captivity at Avignon, the Great Schism when there were three claimants to the papal throne, and watched the moral decline of monasteries and their greedy destruction of farming lands for profiteering in raising sheep. She lived at a time when the Franciscan Friars' fervent promise of reform collapsed and there were the first English heretics in the persons of

John Wyclif and the Lollards. She experienced the uprising of the poor in the Peasants' Revolt and the bitter persecution performed by her own bishop at the Lollard's Pit on the outskirts of Norwich. During her lifetime a king and an archbishop were assassinated, and there were three outbreaks of bubonic plague called the Black Death, which reduced the population of Norwich almost by half.

These catastrophes, which Julian grouped under the collective name of "sin" and which she saw, together with personal offenses, as the results of Adam's sin, are never specifically referred to in her writings. They were very much on her mind, however, and she constantly challenged God to explain how to reconcile such horrors with his loving providence. Indeed, this can be seen as the main thrust of her teachings.

On the thirteenth of May, 1373, Julian received a series of sixteen visions centered on the person and sufferings of Jesus and on the Trinity. A short time later, she wrote an account of them in twenty-five chapters (known as the "Short Text"). Twenty years later, after much prayer and reflection, she wrote another account consisting of eighty-six chapters (called the "Long Text"). During this important interim, Julian the visionary became Julian the theologian.

Julian's visions correspond to the classic understanding of such phenomena. Some visions were spiritual locutions. In this experience, God spoke directly to her heart in such a way as to communicate with absolute, unquestioned clarity the desired message. Actual words were probably not used but the visionary was left with no doubt as to the authenticity or the meaning of the message. Other visions were visual or experienced as coming through the corporeal senses. These resulted from the direct action of God on the imagination. Still others were spiritual visions, not easily expressed and usually concerned with the deeper mysteries of God, such as the Trinity. Many of Julian's visions were combinations of all three types.

SIXTEEN VISIONS

Julian begins her book by giving a sort of table of contents. She lists her sixteen visions, calling them a revelation of love. Eight of these visions are simply given with the briefest of descriptions and eight of them are accompanied by a succinct but profound first attempt at a theological understanding. The first vision, or showing, is the head of Jesus crowned with thorns. This is not to be wondered at, as shortly before, in what was seen as her death throes, the priest held before Julian's failing eyes a crucifix. Julian tells us that contained in this vision was the Trinity, the Incarnation, and the union of the human soul with God. We shall see how Julian was able to relate the Trinity to the activity of each of the three persons in God. We are constantly reminded of Jesus' statement to Philip: "He who sees me sees the Father."

All of the visions that follow from the first one are connected to it and proceed from it.

Julian's observation that this first vision contained teachings of wisdom and love is not to be passed over lightly. The two highest human faculties by which he images God are the intellect and the will. Wisdom is the supreme activity of the intellect, and love is the supreme activity of the will. Herein lies our imaging of God.

The seventh vision is something that Julian experiences more than sees. It is the constant interchange in her life between feelings of well-being and grief. She anticipates here her interpretation of this as a demonstration of the fact that God's goodness preserves us in his love in woe and in well-being. This hints at one of the main themes of Julian's writing, namely, that God's providence overcomes all sin and suffering. The ninth revelation backs this up by paradoxically affirming the joy and delight that the Trinity has in the cruel sufferings of Christ.

Julian develops this in the thirteenth revelation by declaring, for the first time, something often repeated: that God will make all things well that are not well, and we will experience it. The insistence that we will experience it is very comforting and takes the declaration out of the realm of some abstract promise that we may or may not see fulfilled—even though we will have to wait for heaven for the full expression of this experience. In the fourteenth revelation she tells us that God is the foundation of all our prayers. In a sense, our prayers actually come from God. This being so, God will answer them because they are his own and they must be pleasing to him. The sixteenth revelation completes the promise of the first where Julian saw the head of Christ crowned with thorns. She now sees the Trinity enthroned in our souls in the person of Christ Jesus.

&

2

THREE GIFTS AND THREE WOUNDS

As was stated in the Introduction, after writing the Short Text of twenty-five chapters shortly after her visions, Julian spent twenty years praying over and reflecting upon their meaning before she wrote the Long Text. By comparing the two we can see the changes that occurred in Julian's self-image and in her theological maturity. She refers to herself in this chapter as a simple, unlettered creature. This is found only in the Long Text. There is some controversy as to what she meant by "unlettered." Surely, she was not illiterate. Many think she simply meant that she lacked knowledge of Latin or was talking about the unsophisticated state of her education at that time.

Julian provides us with the exact date of her visions: May 13, 1373. She refers to herself deprecatingly (only in the Long Text) as a creature. Clearly, she wishes to minimize her own importance in order to give the emphasis to the message. Sometime previously, she had asked God for three gifts.

In Julian's time devotion to the Passion of our Lord was at its height. Julian, first, asked that she might be given a bodily vision so she could be brought to a greater realization of the sufferings of Jesus. The second gift she requested was to have a mortal illness. Obviously, this was to parallel in her own body the Passion of Jesus, or at least, to be more aware of his sufferings. She wanted to be convinced that she was dying, to receive all the rites of the church, and to have every kind of physical, mental, and spiritual pain that dying involved, except for the actual death itself. She desired this illness not because she wanted to die, but because she wished to live more fervently for the glory of God. Julian knew that these requests were extraordinary and submitted them to God's will.

The third gift she asked for was to receive what she called "three wounds": true contrition, loving compassion, and a longing for God. She emphasizes the importance of a longing for God by stating that the contrition and compassion were eventually forgotten, but never the longing. It is in the Short Text that we see the background behind these wounds. She tells us that she heard a sermon given about St. Cecilia. A Roman Centurion attempted to slay St. Cecilia by decapitation. He attempted three times with his sword, administering three wounds, but was unable to accomplish it. Julian omits this story in the Long Text probably because she did not wish to be seen comparing herself to St. Cecilia.

☒

3

MORTAL ILLNESS

Julian received the illness for which she prayed half way through her thirty-first year. Clearly, her age at this time was to coincide with the supposed age of Christ when he died. We must keep in mind that Julian requested in her prayer that she shouldn't realize that this illness would not be fatal. In other words, she actually was led to think that she was dying. In this way, she could more authentically enter into the experience of Christ in his passion. She mentions that she was quite reluctant to die because she wanted to live longer so she could love God more. Both the pain she suffered and her own reason told her that she would die and that it was God's will.

When Julian experienced this illness she was probably not yet a recluse, as she speaks of the presence of her mother and others at her bedside. In the Long Text she omits a number of minor incidents from the Short Text, such as the cloth that held her head and the small boy carrying the crucifix. After six days, Julian became paralyzed from the middle of her body to her feet. She was helped to sit upright when the priest came. She was staring up into heaven because she thought she was about to go there. The command of the priest to look at the crucifix and be comforted by it made her take her eyes from heaven and focus them on the dying Christ. This is quite significant because it shows that her concern was not how *she* might enter heaven but for the Passion of Christ and the comfort it would offer to her fellow Christians. Her focus on Christ rather than heaven also meant to her that she would live longer. The room around her grew dark but there was still a light on the crucifix. She writes of it as a terrifying ordeal, as though she were in the midst of a crowd of devils.

The paralysis then extended to the upper part of her body. She could hardly breathe and believed she was at the point of death. Then, suddenly, she was free from pain and restored to health. She realized a miracle had occurred; yet somehow she felt that she would rather have died because of her longing for God. This thought reminded her that this was precisely the third of the wounds she had asked for: a longing for God. She saw that the gift of compassion she had also requested would require that she should suffer with him in her living, mortal body, just as he suffered as a mortal man, and that this would lead to a longing for him.

The longing that Julian prayed for is a very important element in the spiritual journey. In its very first chapter, *The Catechism of the Catholic Church* speaks of humankind's capacity for God and the desire for God. Such desire is written in the human heart because humankind is created by God for God and we will find the happiness we search for only in God. As St. Augustine expresses it in the first chapter of his *Confessions*, we are made for God and our hearts are restless until they rest in him. This is eminently true in the mystical journey. The longing that Julian speaks of here can be seen as the equivalent of *attraction*, the first of the four stages of love, so commonly found in the medieval mystics. The longing can also be aligned with St. Bernard's description of the process of love as beginning on a sensible level, then proceeding to the will, and going beyond the will to joy. The longing is physically experienced. Julian realizes its importance even over bodily visions or any other kind of revelation from God.

❧

4

THE FIRST VISION

While Julian looks at the crucifix presented to her by the priest, she suddenly sees blood running down from beneath the crown of thorns. It is a very realistic vision and she describes the blood as hot and flowing copiously. Julian will later tell us that this first vision was connected to all the subsequent ones that, as it were, flowed from it. Thus, we see in the vision the sources of some of the most important themes in Julian's writings.

As frequently happens in mystical experiences, this vision takes on the quality of a spiritual rather than a physical occurrence—something that indicates that the vision has the kind of great depth usually associated with the mystery of the Trinity or, sometimes, our Lady St. Mary. The vision notes Julian happened suddenly, and we get the impression that it occurred simultaneously with the bleeding head of Jesus.

In the hierarchy of truths that the Church teaches, the doctrine of the Trinity is the most important. It is God's revelation of God's self touching upon his inmost nature in a manner and concerning a matter that could not be known through natural reasoning. Julian is given to understand and, indeed, to experience the Trinity as our creator, preserver, lover, and endless joy. The Trinity for her is by no means a theological abstraction, and it is through the Passion of Christ that she receives and understands it. In all of her subsequent visions regarding the Passion of Christ, Julian will see Christ in the Trinity and the Trinity in him.

Julian now introduces another theme: namely, that she received these visions not just for herself but for others. In fact, Julian minimizes her own role by stating her awe at the realization that one who is so revered could be so intimate with such a wretch as she.

Julian realizes that the joy she is receiving is a special gift from the Lord to be a source of strength before her death when she will be tempted by devils. Again, Julian acknowledges that her visions were given her for the sake of others, who would also be comforted by the Trinity and the Passion of Christ against their spiritual enemies at the time of death.

Finally, Julian initiates another of her important themes: the motherhood of God. She does this somewhat indirectly by stating that she had a spiritual vision or understanding of our Lady St. Mary, as a simple, humble creature who was, at the same time, through her humility, God's greatest creation, second only to the humanity of Christ. Julian is given this understanding in connection with the Passion of Christ because through his passion, as she will later explain, Christ bestows upon us his mothering nurture and love.

ø

5

THE HAZELNUT

In this chapter, Julian experiences all three types of visions. While she is still having the bodily vision of the bleeding head of Christ, she is also given a spiritual vision corresponding to the deepest mysteries of God and, at the same time, is given spiritual locutions to help her understand these visions. She also has two additional bodily visions of great symbolic import. She is about to deal with an understanding of a deep theological and philosophical depth, touching on the very nature of God's being. First, however, she is prepared by a warm experience of God's intimate love bestowed on her as though it were some kind of personal, comfortable clothing embracing and wrapping her in its love. She is given to understand that everything that is good is contained in God and God in it. This is to prepare us for the negative approach to God she is about to consider.

What follows is perhaps the most well known of Julian's visions: the hazelnut. What Julian actually sees is a small round ball, no bigger than a hazelnut, in the palm of her hand. It is so small and fragile that she wonders how it could possibly continue to exist. She marvels greatly as to its meaning and is given to understand that it is, indeed, the entire cosmos. We are reminded here of the vision of St. Benedict who saw all creation in the mote of a sunbeam or of the poet William Blake, who saw the universe in a grain of sand. However, for Julian this is not a metaphysical experience but a personal awareness, on a contemplative level, of what John of the Cross expressed when he says: "Nothing, nothing, nothing." This is as close as Julian gets to speaking of the *via negativa*, the negative way to God, favored by the author of the *Cloud of Unknowing* (hereafter called *The Cloud*) as opposed to the *via positiva*, the positive way to God, favored by Walter Hilton, both of whom were contemporaries of Julian.

Julian is involved here in a paradox. All created things are as nothing in themselves without God. Unless God's continuing love upholds them they will cease to exist. How ridiculous it is then to place our trust in anything less than God! Julian wants to teach us the littleness of all created things, but, at the same time, she is careful to end the chapter by assuring us that all creation is filled with God's goodness. Nonetheless, we must come to him devoid of attachment to any created thing. We must seek to approach God as true mystics, that is, without any intermediaries. This is reminiscent of *The Cloud*, which speaks of the contemplative experience as a naked intent toward God.

Julian, with great insight and wisdom, speaks of the futility of seeking anything less than God. In our prayers we should always realize that what we ultimately seek is God no matter what we are ostensibly asking for. Anything else would be like asking for that little hazelnut.

♇

6

INTERMEDIARIES IN PRAYER

In the negative way that Julian is familiar with, we are taught that contemplative prayer requires that we bury all thoughts, images, memories, ideas, and imaginations and go directly and immediately to God without the use of such intermediaries. This is an advanced form of prayer and is quite different from what we are accustomed to—the ordinary way of prayer, sometimes called discursive prayer. This prayer involves the use of the intellect and so we consciously use thoughts, memories, and ideas, which Julian refers to here as intermediaries. Julian tells us that in the highest prayer (i.e., contemplation), we do not use these intermediaries but rather go directly to God. His goodness is all we need to be drawn to him and to cling to him.

What may be momentarily shocking to us is when Julian specifies what these intermediaries usually are. They involve any created thing—even the humanity of Christ, the graciousness of the Blessed Virgin, and the intercession of the saints that God has given us for our salvation. They are all products or manifestations of the goodness of God, and in our highest form of prayer we go directly to this goodness in itself without the need of them. This prayer is an act of the loving will cleaving directly and nakedly to God, surpassing the knowledge or ability of any created thing to express.

Julian is not through with shocking us. The imagery that she uses next in the text is about as fundamental and basic as it could possibly be. A man stands upright, puts food in his mouth like someone opening a purse to insert an object, then when the time is right, he disposes of this digested food as though through another opening in the bottom of the purse, which is then closed until needed again! Julian sees this as an image of God coming down to us to provide for our most basic physical functions. God honors what he has created, even in the most fundamental needs of the body, because of his love for our soul created in his image. Also, in spite of the contemplative's independence from all intermediaries, the latter are, nonetheless, God-filled creatures and signs of his goodness. The heart is clothed in the breast, the bones in the flesh, the flesh in the skin, and the skin is clad in the clothing. But this, Julian states, will all pass away. God, our Lover, desires that we cleave immediately to his goodness, which will never pass away. No intermediary, no created thing, can possibly express the extent of God's love. Only contemplation can approach God's unspeakable love in wonder and in awe.

Julian's theological understanding here is profound. Everything we can desire and ask our Lord for simply directs us to him. Any desire we have is intended to lead to yet higher desire, and this will continue until we reach the highest desire of all in the fullness of joy. This teaching is the base for all the visions that will follow. Humility—knowledge of the truth of one's self—is foundational for the knowledge of God, which is true humility and results in an overflowing of love for all men and women. Julian does not want us to see contemplation as "naval gazing." Awe leads to love, which leads to joy, which leads to service of God and neighbor.

ℬ

7

GOD IS MOST COURTEOUS

Our Lady St. Mary was filled by God with humility. This, along with love, is the contemplative virtue. Her wisdom and knowledge of the truth led her to perfect humility. There was nothing of the false self in her that would interfere with her contemplation of the goodness of God.

Along with her spiritual vision, Julian continues to have a bodily vision of the bleeding head of Christ. The forms the blood takes are important symbols. It falls in great abundance like water from the eaves of a house during the rain. The drops are also round like pellets and as they spread over the forehead, they flatten out like the scales of a fish. All this makes the vision hideous, vivid, and, at the same time, lovely. Julian understands that this means three things: God is to be revered and feared, God is gracious and courteous, and God fills the soul with certainty and joy.

In spite of her earlier reference to herself as illiterate, it is obvious that Julian was well-trained in the systematic, scholastic philosophy/theology of her day. However, her thinking was not left-brained, linear, systematic, or merely logical. She was, rather, right-brained, metaphorical, and intuitive. In accordance with the systematic philosophy of scholasticism, Julian understood God to be Perfect Act. This meant that God was totally perfect, all-wise, all-powerful, and, at every moment, fully exercising, in an active unlimited manner, all of his infinite potential. Because Julian expresses this in her intuitive, right-brain manner she is able to attribute to God all manner of paradoxes. Thus, God can be totally other and closely intimate at the same time. Julian manifests this in the following allegory.

Julian is given a homely vision that anticipates the allegory of the Lord and the servant in chapter 51, which is probably her most important vision. The greatest honor a king can do for a poor servant is to be courteous to him, to treat him personally and intimately with courtly graciousness, in an open and public way, so that this kind of a gift would be far more significant than any particular item, no matter how great its value. This majestic, yet intimate familiarity would give the servant such joy that he would almost forget his own existence. This is the experience of the contemplative mystic.

So it is that the Lord Jesus, who is highest and noblest, is at the same time the humblest and most courteous. The Lord does this to give us hope. Julian wishes this hope to be seen as a Trinitarian experience. The wonderful familiarity is from the Father, our Creator, in our Lord Jesus Christ, who is our brother, and from an abundance of grace given by the Holy Spirit. The three theological virtues of faith, hope, and love, which are God's means of communicating God's self to us, will remain with us until the end of our lives. It also speaks of the fullness of what God has planned for us in unending love in heaven.

ℬ

8

NOT FOR JULIAN

Carried away by the love she experienced by way of her vision of the bleeding head of Christ, Julian is compelled to express it out loud by the words "Blessed be God." *The Cloud* speaks of such spontaneous vocalizations by experienced contemplatives. Julian follows this with a clear and precise review of her interpretation and understanding from this first vision. She interprets six things: a sign of the Passion; the Mother of God; the powerful, wise, and loving Trinity; that everything God has created is ample and good but appears so little in his presence; all is created and upheld by love; and finally, that God is everything that is good and the goodness that everything has is God.

At that moment, Julian writes, the bodily vision ceases but the spiritual sight remains in her understanding. She earnestly desires to understand even more. And in all of this she is moved in love toward her fellow Christians because she understands that this vision is being shown for them. Julian was sure that her death was imminent and she wanted it to be an inspiring example of love for those around her. Just as her vision was meant for those who would live after her death, she wanted her very death to be for them an example of love. This was a primary duty of an anchoress: to live and die for her fellow Christians, as expressed in a rule of life for recluses, the *Ancrene Riwle*, which Julian surely read.

In this and in the following chapter, Julian clearly states a fundamental principle of her teaching. The Lord intended all of her spiritual showings not for Julian personally, but for all her fellow Christians. This is probably the reason why there is such scarcity of information about Julian's personal life in the book. Julian then makes a dramatic appeal to her readers to accept her vision for their own reassurance and their great joy because God has shown it for them. Some theologians, for this reason, hold Julian's revelations to be something more than private—that somehow they partake of the nature of public revelation, which formally ceased with the death of the last apostle. At any rate, it is a great consolation, experienced by all readers of Julian's work, to know that it was written for them as expressly willed by God.

⌀

9

LOVE UNITES ALL

This is truly a beautiful chapter with a beautiful message. Julian points out that the fact that she has received visions does not make her holy. She is only holy to the extent that these visions bring her to love God better. Their purpose is to bring strength and comfort to the simple who may never have had revelations or visions but only the common teaching of the Church, and who may very well love God more than she does.

Julian explains here what may very well be the highest expression of her teaching. She does not pay special attention to herself but rather to the unity of love that she has with her fellow Christians. Unity, or *oneing*, in love is the sum and substance of Julian's soteriology, her understanding of salvation. Her teaching here is very similar to that of *The Cloud*. When we are united (one'd) to God in love, we are then united in love to all whom God is united.

When we unpack the meaning of that statement it means that we are in love with all creation. We are united in love with everything God has made. We are united with every man, woman, and child who ever existed since the creation of the world, who exists today, and even who will exist in the future. Our love extends to the utmost limits of the cosmos. It reaches into dimensions of reality that we do not even know exist. It is the very love of God.

But what about those who are not saved? Julia now touches upon a very delicate subject that is a matter of some controversy. She speaks of being united in love with all those who will be saved. She then uses a somewhat evasive figure of speech that she will repeat toward the end of her book when addressing the same subject. She says that she was given to see only those who would be saved and that God did not give her to see anyone else. Does this mean that there was no one else? Or does she mean that she was simply not given any information about anyone else?

Julian insists here, as she does later, that she is a faithful daughter of the Church and believes everything that Holy Church preaches and teaches. Why does she consistently juxtapose her protestation of being an orthodox believer with a pointed silence about the possibility of someone being condemned to hell? For the systematic theologian this would violate the rules of logic; but what does it mean for Julian, who maintains that she contemplated her revelations as God intended? She concludes this chapter by repeating the classic understanding of the three types of visions: bodily vision, locutions, and spiritual understanding. The spiritual understandings (Was this one? About the existence of hell?), she maintains, she cannot show as fully as she should wish!

≫

10

GOD IN MAN'S IMAGE

In Julian's second vision she looks directly into the face of the crucifix that hangs before her. Her sight of the blood on Jesus' face seems to confuse her as though the light on it is not adequate. She is given a spiritual locution telling her that she needs no other light than God and, whether she is given the light or not, it is up to God. Julian projects this experience and understanding into daily life where she sees God, seeks God, possesses God, and then lacks God. This, she said, is how it should be.

God wants us to believe that we see him continually. It may seem to us that this sight is only partial, like the dim vision of the face of the crucifix. But no matter where we are, even if we were at the bottom of the sea, we would come to no harm if we could only realize that God is continuously with us.

Julian is distressed at the inadequacy of this second vision, which seemed to her to be so small and simple that she wonders if it was, indeed, a revelation at all. The Lord, however, gave her to understand that it was so. It was dim and inadequate because it symbolized the Lord's death. It reminds Julian of the face imprinted on Veronica's veil, a relic she believed to be held in Rome. How could this image of one so fair as the Lord be so ugly? There can be little doubt but that Julian's imagery here refers to the Black Death. In her typical fashion, Julian juxtaposes her images without specifically stating their connection; it is up to the reader to draw from them what Julian would call a second sight. As Jesus imprinted his likeness on Veronica's veil, so he imprints it on the faces of those who suffered from the plague. Jesus suffers in us in the plague and in all that it represents in sin, suffering, and death. He transforms its ugliness by giving to it the likeness of his beautiful face.

This is what she is given to understand: The Trinity created humankind in their image and likeness. When humankind sinned and lost this image, only the Trinity could restore it. Humankind was restored by the same love in which he was created. Just as in our first creation, we were made in the image of the Trinity, so in our restoration we are remade in the image of Jesus Christ. On the other hand, when the Lord became human, he wanted to be as much like that wretched creature as possible, in all things except sin. So he took on humankind's foul image and likeness, which included even his death. This was the meaning of this vision of death, so dim and so ugly.

It is made clear to Julian that we will always receive safety and comfort, even if we are at the very bottom of the sea, so long as we comprehend that God is with us. God wants us to believe that he is always with us. He wishes to be seen, sought, awaited, and trusted. When the soul seeks God, it pleases God very much. The soul manifests faith, hope, and love and realizes that, in times of distress, seeking God is as good as beholding him. He will teach the soul what to do for his greater glory. Clinging to God with trust honors him whether we actually see him or not. We should seek God diligently and joyfully, steadfastly and without grumbling, trusting that he will reveal himself according to his simple and gracious will.

⌀

II

No Sin

Julian's next vision is to see God in an instant. Her understanding, however, was to expand and behold God's infinite wisdom, power, and goodness. Philosophically, in this chapter she is speaking of God as Perfect Act. God alone is the creator and the mover of all that is. This being so, everything that is, is good, and everything that is done is good. It follows, therefore, that nothing is evil. From our point of view, we see things done by luck or chance, but from God's point of view everything proceeds from infinite wisdom, power, and love. Whenever Julian uses these three words—power, wisdom and love—we know that she is referring to the Trinity.

Although Julian does not quote it, we are reminded in this chapter of St. Paul's letter to the Romans, where he maintains that God's foolishness and weakness are stronger and wiser than our power and wisdom. Like that of all the great mystics, the basis for Julian's belief is that we live in the most perfect of all worlds. Nothing is done by luck or chance but only by the all-foreseeing wisdom of God.

Julian does admit that, from humankind's point of view, there is chaos, chance, and sin; however, here she is speaking only from God's point of view. Julian realizes that sin is the absence of due good, but that is far too abstract for her right-brain thinking. Everything is well done and God sees that it is good. At another time, she will be given to see sin from our point of view, but even this is given to her that she may understand the mercy and love of God.

This chapter is foundational for an understanding of Julian's great cry of joy, "Everything shall be well."

⌀

12

THE FOURTH REVELATION

Julian's next vision is that of the scourging of Jesus. The realism of her description of the flowing of his precious blood may be a bit too intense for the modern reader. However, even the realism is a part of the symbolism. Julian stresses the copiousness of the flow. Her vision flows over into reality when she says that the blood was so abundant that, if it were actually to happen, it would soak her bed and the surrounding area.

Such a vision had a significant influence on her reflections, as we shall see. It reminded her of the abundance of water with which God blesses the earth for our physical well-being. God does this out of love; but even more so does he rain down the power of the precious blood of Jesus. The blood is given us to drink in the Eucharist.

The imagery of its abundance flowing from the body of Jesus is carried over into the image of the blood of Jesus pouring into the realm of the dead, overflowing the earth to wash away sins, and ascending into heaven in the risen body of Jesus where it will forever flow in the presence of the Father, rejoicing in our salvation.

ꙮ

13

THE FIFTH REVELATION

Julian's fifth revelation comes in the form of an interior locution. She hears it clearly in her heart even though not a word is spoken. This is a difficult chapter, involving, as it does, the devil as a positive, personal entity on whom the medieval mind delighted in casting scorn, woe, and suffering. Julian is aware that evil was caused not only by the devil, but also by the world and the flesh. She is also conscious of evil philosophically as a lack of due being. Nevertheless, she prefers to attribute it personally to the fiend.

The words spoken in the depths of her soul tell her that the passion of our Lord has overcome the devil. Julian speaks of "those who will be saved" frequently. Is she saying, by implication, that there are also those who will not be saved; or is she using this phrase as a means of avoiding any declarative affirmation that there are none who will be condemned? At any rate, Julian assures us that the devil receives no joy in his work, whether or not it is successful. Also in God there is no wrath, even for the devil. Rather it is God's power and justice that withstands him. Julian then seems to contradict herself because she maintains that this God, who seems to be beyond emotion, scorns the devil. Possibly, by *scorns* she means *ignores.*

This thought causes such joy within Julian that it wells up into outright laughter, causing those standing around her bed to laugh also. (It is information such as this that prompts us to believe that Julian experienced these visions before she was a recluse.) Julian is careful to remark that she did not see Christ laughing, even though he was responsible for her laughter by giving her this understanding. By doing this, Christ demonstrates the inward constancy consistent with his Passion.

Following her penchant for expressing things in threes (no doubt because of her Trinitarian framework), Julian sees three qualities in this revelation: amusement that the devil is conquered; scorn, as God scorns him; and seriousness, because it was brought about by the labor of Christ's passion.

☙

14

THE SIXTH REVELATION

B ecause of her conviction that her visions were given to her for the sake of all men and women, Julian does not inform us of any particular situations she has experienced in her own life that might have occasioned one or other of them. It is not unreasonable to surmise that the vision of this chapter might be intended for those of her fellow Christians who have lost young children, possibly to the plague. Thus, Julian informs us that the ages of those whom God rewards in heaven are known to all, and that even a very brief time in God's service receives the same threefold reward as a lifetime.

Heaven is seen as a banquet in the house of the king. The king does not limit himself to a throne-room but rather seems to be present throughout the entire mansion, gracefully and gratefully giving himself equally to all of his guests, young and old. Three degrees of happiness are given to all. The first degree is God's gratitude. This alone is so sublime that it is adequate recompense for a lifetime of pain and suffering. The second comes from this honor being recognized by all the souls in heaven. The third is that the honor and favor that God bestows on his beloved will last forever.

❧

15

THE SEVENTH REVELATION

What a truly marvelous instruction for the spiritual journey we are given in this chapter! God, out of love, visits us ultimately with comfort and joy, then sorrow and affliction. The affliction need not arise from personal sins nor does the comfort proceed from merit. Both are directed by God's love. The times of comfort and joy are welcome and spiritual and need no further supports. The periods of affliction, however, can be sustained only by faith, hope, and love without sensible consolation. God wishes us to realize that, whether we are in comfort or in sorrow, he keeps us safe.

Julian describes the sorrow in distress as being left to ourselves. This is how God humbles us: that we may realize the truth of all our inadequacies and open our minds and hearts to the knowledge and love of God. This is standard advice given by any spiritual director. What follows, however, is unique to Julian. We must not give in to sorrow and suffering for they are passing. We should do all in our power to preserve the times of consolation because bliss lasts forever!

❧

16

THE EIGHTH REVELATION

In this and in the next chapter, Julian gives us a pain-filled description of the final moments of Christ's Passion. It is unpleasant, graphic, and overly realistic. We must recall, however, as stated in the second chapter, that Julian had desired a bodily sight of the savior's physical pains. She desired this because it would enable her to be united with the Passion in her own sufferings, to understand its meaning, and to allow it to be transformed into joy.

Julian places great emphasis on the pain caused by the Lord's body being dried up through loss of blood and by anguish. There were also external factors such as a bitter, cold, dry wind. It looked to Julian as though he had been dead for a week. The drying of his flesh was his last and greatest pain.

⌀

17

THE HOLY THIRST

In the course of the revelations, Christ's words came to Julian's mind: "I thirst." She recognizes this thirst as being both physical and spiritual. She reserves her observations on the spiritual thirst for chapter 31 where she will relate it to her great prayer that all will be well. For now, she continues her graphic description of the physical sufferings of the Lord, including the effect of the crown of thorns on Jesus' flesh and the nails in his hands and feet.

Although Julian realizes that Christ suffered his Passion only once, during the revelations he is now sharing it with her (and all her fellow Christians). The pain she feels is so great that she regrets having asked to experience it. This causes her to reflect on the pains of hell. Her pain is physical and temporary and caused by her love of the savior, while the torments of hell are different especially because of the despair that accompanied them. During this experience, Julian's love for the savior is so great that her worst pain is the sorrow she feels for his agony. She is now preparing for a transfer from suffering to love and to give us an understanding that the motive for Christ's Passion was not sin but love.

✍

18

UNITED IN THE PASSION

J ulian is now to experience the fulfillment of her prayer in chapter 3: knowledge of the bodily pains of the savior (seen in the last chapter), knowledge of the compassion of our Lady, and that of all his true lovers. Julian sees that St. Mary's natural love for her son was enhanced by grace; the corresponding pain she suffered was greater than any others because her love was greater. The disciples and the other followers of Christ experienced more agony than they did at their own deaths. This leads Julian to an understanding of the great oneness (unity) between Christ and all her fellow Christians brought about through the sufferings of Christ.

Julian notes that all creation joined in that suffering and the very heavens and earth were unable to function because of sorrow. When Christ, through whom everything was made, failed, so did they. Even those who did not recognize Christ experienced suffering, as the comforts of all creation were denied them. Two persons can symbolize those who did not recognize Christ: Pilate and St. Denis of France. Julian here refers to a third-century French martyr confused in the popular tradition with Dionysius the Areopagite, who in Acts chapter 17 was converted by St. Paul in Athens when Paul preached on "the unknown God." God, who has given us the blessed and accursed, the planets and the elements, withdrew their functioning so that those who recognized him and those who did not were in sorrow at that time. In Julian's understanding of salvation all things are one'd (united) in the passion of Christ.

⌀

19

THE CROSS IS THE WAY

In the revelations, Julian wanted to look away from the cross but she realized that as long as she contemplated the cross she was safe. Apart from the cross, there was no way to be safe from the devil. She was soon to realize, however, that the flesh would also tempt her. This came in the form of a seemingly friendly voice telling her to look up to the Father in heaven. Julian realized that if she did this, she would see nothing between the cross and heaven, which might interfere with her progress there. Nonetheless, she could not take her eyes away. She knew then that the cross was her heaven, no matter how painful it might be. For her, it was the only way to heaven.

At that time, Julian saw Jesus only in pain. Nonetheless, she chose him for her heaven. That she did this, she writes, had always been a comfort to her and taught her to choose only Jesus in joy and sorrow. Once again, Julian recalls that she regretted having asked to be united to Jesus in his Passion. This was the call of the flesh to which she did not give the assent of her soul and so it was not imputed to her as sin. She experienced, at the same time, a positive and negative response that she calls reluctance and deliberate choice. The flesh was reluctant, but the heart was willing. Her heart made a choice that Julian expresses in her customary Trinitarian formula: powerfully, wisely, and with a full, loving will, she chose Jesus for her heaven. It was shown to her that the Spirit would draw the flesh by grace; it was not shown to her that the opposite could happen. Again Julian uses her favorite circumlocution to make an affirmation that might otherwise be shocking to her readers.

✑

20

SPIRIT STRENGTHENS THE FLESH

Julian has just maintained that the Spirit strengthens the flesh. In this chapter, she applies this again on a new level. The divinity of the Lord gives strength to his humanity and so he is able to suffer more than normal humans could. The higher his dignity was, the greater the depth of his suffering. It is most important that we understand that he who underwent the passion is God. Then we must consider what he suffered and for whom.

Christ gave Julian to understand, albeit imperfectly, the exaltedness of his divinity, the vulnerability of his humanity, and his reluctance to suffer pain. As he suffered for our sins, so he sorrowed for our desolation out of his compassionate love. Even though he has risen from the dead and is no longer subject to suffering, paradoxically, he suffers with us. (Julian is to develop this thought at greater length in another chapter.) Great love endures great suffering and great suffering produces great joy. Julian ends chapter 20 by saying that we should contemplate the Passion in three ways, the first of which is with sorrow and compassion. It is not clear in the next chapter what the other two ways are, but Julian will take them up in chapter 22.

✑

21

THE NINTH REVELATION

When Julian was dying and, indeed, seemed at the point of death, she was suddenly and miraculously restored to health. As she looked at the cross, her sorrow was changed into joy. She must have been recalling this when she had the ninth revelation. Jesus seemed to be at the point of death when, suddenly, his appearance changed to one of joy, which Julian immediately shared. The Lord spoke to her mind and asked her if any vestige of her pain or grief remained. She understood this to mean that we are now on the cross with him, suffering and dying with him. However, at the last moment of life, suddenly, he will change his appearance for us and we will be with him in the joy of heaven. For the little pain we suffered in this life we shall have an eternal knowledge in God.

ℒ

22

THREE HEAVENS

In this chapter, Julian describes one of the deepest kinds of spiritual vision, involving the Trinity. Like many other chapters, chapter 22 is completely Trinitarian, even to the extent of Julian's method of expressing herself constantly in threes. The chapter also reveals a refreshingly unique way of looking at the Passion of our Lord. We always consider the Passion from our point of view, pondering on how it affects us, our guilt feelings because of it, our lack of gratitude, our sins that caused it and our salvation that results from it. Julian, however, considers it from the point of view of Jesus, as an act of love.

Jesus begins with a strange question, asking Julian if she is well satisfied with his suffering for her. If she is satisfied, so is he. If it were possible for God to suffer even more, he would gladly do so. Julian's response to this is to be lifted up into heaven in her understanding. She sees three heavens or three states of bliss. In this chapter, she speaks of the first two. As we might expect, the three heavens are related to the three persons of the Trinity. Consequently, all three heavens are equal to one another in their joy

In the first bliss or heaven, Julian sees the Father in Christ, not through a bodily vision but by way of his attributes. The Father's operation in this heaven is to reward his Son because he is well pleased with what Jesus has done for our salvation. Thus, we belong to Jesus not only because he has redeemed us but also because of his Father's gracious gift. We are Jesus' bliss, reward, honor, and especially his crown. Jesus receives such joy from the Father that he counts as nothing his own suffering and death. Julian is given to understand that Jesus would die for us over and over again if it were possible. However, because his humanity could suffer only once, his goodness can never stop offering it to the Father.

Julian now returns to a theme she began in chapter 21: the three ways of viewing the Passion. She now refers to the second way. As far as the heavens are above the earth, the love that made Jesus suffer his passion is above all other sufferings. This suffering was noble, precious, and honorable, performed only once through his love, but this love is without beginning and shall be without end. It proceeded from the wisdom of God and could not have been planned more perfectly. As a result, it brought to Jesus complete joy.

☧

23

JOY, BLISS AND DELIGHT

Julian's Trinitarian framework gets ever more intense. By saying that Christ's passion is a joy, she means that the Father was pleased. By saying that it was bliss, she means that the Son was honored, and by saying that it was endless delight, she refers to the Holy Spirit. What a remarkable way Julian offers us to consider the passion of Christ! She then refers back to another Trinitarian reference: namely, the three ways of viewing the passion. She has already mentioned the first way, which is that we should behold his cruel sufferings with compassion. The second way is that the love that made Jesus suffer surpasses all of his sufferings. The third way is to see the joy and the bliss that made the Father take delight in the Lord's Passion.

Julian now reviews the five visions she has had of the Lord's suffering; the bleeding head, the discoloration of his blessed face, the abundant bleeding of his body from the scourging, the excessive drying out of his body, and finally, the joy of his passion. It is this fifth vision that she wishes to emphasize now. God wants us to share delight with him in our salvation and to receive strength and comfort from it because we are his bliss. Here, Julian spontaneously breaks forth in prayer to Jesus that our delight in our salvation be like the joy that Jesus has in it.

The Passion of the Lord is the work of the Trinity. Only the humanity of Christ suffered and the Trinity took joy in it. This is what God means when he asks Julian if she is satisfied, and that if she is then Christ is satisfied. Julian then, without specifically quoting it, comments on St. Paul's statement in 2 Corinthians 9:7: "The Lord loves a cheerful giver." For Julian, the Trinity is the cheerful giver who pays little attention to the gift as long as he can please and comfort the one who receives it. Again, in the Trinitarian framework, Julian mentions three joys coming from the passion: Christ rejoices because he will suffer no more, he has redeemed us from hell, and he has brought us up into heaven as his everlasting bliss and crown.

ℒ

24

THE TENTH REVELATION

This revelation was both bodily and spiritual. Jesus looked into the wound in his side and drew Julian's understanding in with him. In a self-effacing manner, Julian here refers to herself as his creature. In the revelation, Jesus showed her a place large enough for all humankind. He reminded her of the blood and water that he shed for love. At the same time, he showed her his blessed heart split in two and joyfully revealed to her understanding something of his divinity. Julian anticipates here the devotion to the Sacred Heart.

Jesus speaks to Julian with joy and love in endearing terms as a brother and calls her his dear one and his child. Jesus loved her so much that he died for her and suffered willingly as much as he could, thus changing his pain to endless joy, both for her and for himself. Because of this, he would gladly grant to Julian anything she asked for. He did all of this, Julian says to her fellow Christians, to show how he loves them and to make them happy.

ℒ

25

THE ELEVENTH REVELATION

Following her priorities, Julian speaks first of the Trinity, then the divinity of Christ, then our Lady St. Mary. Even when Julian speaks of our Lady, she does so in a Trinitarian framework, expressing much of it in triplets. She is called sweet maiden, blessed mother, our Lady. She has an exalted, wondrous, special love. She is high, noble, and worthy. Her virtues are in truth, wisdom, and love.

When Julian speaks of the Trinity, she is sharing the understanding that she receives from a spiritual revelation rather than a bodily one. Likewise, here she is not given a bodily revelation of St. Mary but a spiritual sight of her virtues. Previously, Julian had seen her as little and simple but now she is viewed as noble and glorious. In giving this revelation to Julian and to her fellow Christians, the Lord took great joy. He showed our Lady St. Mary three times: as she was conceived, as she was beneath the cross, and as she is now in honor and bliss. All of this resulted from Jesus gazing into the wound in his side. In other words, it came as an expression of the deep love in his heart, which was vast and open.

✄

26

THE TWELFTH REVELATION: I AM

Julian packs so much meaning into this brief chapter that she is unable to explain it further. It surpasses all that her heart could think or her soul could desire. She alludes here to God's revelation of himself to Moses as *I Am* and to the *I Am* sayings of Jesus from the Gospel of St. John. Jesus says: "I am he, I am he whom you love, I am he who is your bliss, I am he who is all" again and again, until he has compiled a list of ten attributes. Once again, Julian demonstrates that she favors the *via positiva*—speaking of God through what he is—rather than the *via negativa*—speaking of God through what he is not.

⌀

27

THE THIRTEENTH REVELATION

In this revelation, the Lord reminds Julian how she had longed for him in the past and she muses that, if it weren't for sin, we would all be as pure as we were when the Lord first created the human race. This causes her to wonder why God, who was all-knowing, did not prevent sin from the beginning. Then all would be well! Even though she knows that such thinking was indiscreet, Julian grieves because of this state of affairs.

The Lord answers her with that powerful statement for which Julian is so well known: everything *will* be well, and every kind of thing will be well. Then the Lord says something that, on first sight, seems shocking, but which is verified time and again through the scriptures: sin is necessary! By "sin," Julian understands Christ to mean all of the evil let loose on the earth since Adam's sin, especially the Passion of Christ and our share in that Passion through our own sufferings. We cannot help but be reminded here of the prayer from the Easter Vigil: "O necessary sin of Adam which brought us such a wonderful savior."

In the revelation, Julian is shown in a moment of time that the Passion of Christ was the greatest of all pains. The Lord quickly

31

consoles her as she realizes that she has never actually seen sin (evil). Julian, here, becomes more philosophical by stating that sin has no real being and can only be recognized by the pain that comes from it. Pain is only temporary and cleanses us and makes us humble so that we will ask for God's mercy. The Passion of the Lord, the greatest pain of all, is given to us as a comfort to show us the Lord's love. It is true, the Lord tells us, that sin is the cause of all pain but, nonetheless, every kind of thing will be well. Julian here makes an observation that the Lord showed her this revelation without manifesting any blame to her or to any of her fellow Christians. She will take this up later, most beautifully, in the parable of the lord and the servant. God does not look upon us with blame. As Julian will later say, he sees us with pity, not with blame.

There follows one of the great controversies in Julian's writings. What is not explicitly said here but which should be understood is the question of hell: an eternity of suffering. If God imputes no blame to anyone because of sin, why should there be a hell? In heaven we shall share with the Lord the mystery behind evil: why it is permitted. This knowledge will make us rejoice forever. We shall see later Julian's mysterious reconciliation between the teaching on hell and the Lord's promise that everything will be well.

☙

28

UNITED WITH CHRIST

This chapter could be seen as a mini homily in which Julian encapsulates the essence of her teaching. It can be summarized in the words of St. Paul: "Make up in your body what is lacking in the sufferings of Christ." The particular sufferings that Julian focuses on, however, in this chapter are the sufferings that result from the scandals in the Church. This is yet another reason why Julian is a mystic for our day. Faithful Christians suffer grievously at the scandals in today's Church; it was, possibly, even worse in Julian's time. The pomp and circumstance of the world had infected the Church's hierarchy. The Franciscans, once seen to be the hope of the Church, were in moral decline, and there were as many as three anti-popes competing for the papal throne. England was infested with heresies, possibly for the first time, in the form of the Lollards.

All of this filled Julian with compassion for her fellow creatures. God's servants in the Church, she writes, will be shaken like a cloth in the wind. All of this demonstrates the truth the Lord has spoken to Julian: that sin is necessary. He does not impute blame but rather pity. His Passion is the place of union with the sufferings of all his people and it has the capacity to turn these sufferings to joy. Jesus says to his people just what the Father said to the Jews: that he will shatter them because of their sins but then he will gather them together, humble and pure, united to himself.

It is to be noted that Julian's use of scripture is by allusion rather than direct quotes. Also, quite possibly, her knowledge of scripture is mainly taken from the liturgy, the Divine Office and the Eucharist, rather than directly from the Bible.

∅

29

NOT CONVINCED

Amazingly, it seems that the consoling statements that Our Lord revealed to her did not convince Julian. She continued to grieve because of the great harm she saw resulting from sin. How could all things possibly be well? She needed further explanation.

In the course of the revelation, Our Lord gently responds by stating a clear teaching of the Church: that Adam's sin was the most harmful activity ever performed. Yet the reparation that Jesus offered was all the more powerful because of it. Because the Lord made all things well, even in spite of Adam's sin, he clearly could make all things well that were less than that.

ℬ

30

TWO UNDERSTANDINGS

The Lord then graces Julian with two insights. The first is clear and open: Our portion is the Lord and salvation. We are taught this by the Church and by the Holy Spirit and Our Lord wants us to be concerned with this and rejoice in it. The second insight is that there is something hidden from us. It goes beyond our personal salvation and God chooses to keep it private. Julian alludes here to the petition in the Lord's Prayer: "Thy will be done on earth as it is in heaven." She says that the saints in heaven wish only for God's will, and wish to know nothing more than God wills them to know. Julian says there are those who occupy themselves in speculating on things they should not know according to God's will. God has compassion on them but prefers that they would occupy themselves in the Lord and trust him for everything. Is Julian here referring to the question of hell? Is she saying that we should leave the issue alone and let God handle it?

ℬ

31

ALL THINGS WELL

The Lord answers all Julian's questions by saying that he may, can, and will make all things well. Again, reverting to her Trinitarian framework, Julian notes that "I may" refers to the Father, "I can" refers to the Son, and "I will" refers to the Holy Spirit. When the Lord says, "I shall," it refers to the Trinity, three persons in one truth. We will see this for ourselves.

God wants us to be at peace in his promise. Jesus thirsts for us in his love, which will endure until we are all gathered together on the last day into his endless joy. Is Julian speaking here about universal salvation? She speaks elsewhere (chapter 32) very clearly about those who will be condemned to an eternity in hell. It seems that she is being pulled in two directions, both of which have equal force. The Church clearly teaches the existence of hell, but her loving God—Father, Son, and Holy Spirit—clearly teaches that all manner of things will be well. We are simply going to have to wait until heaven and see for ourselves how this will come about. Right now, it is God's secret and that should satisfy us. She will attempt to resolve this further in the next chapter.

⌀

32

A SECRET ACT

This is certainly the most controversial of all of the chapters in Julian's work. To fathom its true meaning, we must break the boundaries of systematic logic and left-brain thinking. The Lord has promised Julian that she will see for herself that all things will be well. This promise provides Julian with two insights. The Lord holds in his providence all things great and small and he includes them in his statement that all things will be well. Nothing will be forgotten, whether it is noble or simple. We see evil things done and it seems impossible that any good could come of them. We think of them with sorrow because we are blind and stupid and cannot see God's wisdom and power and goodness in them. This is key to Julian's understanding of hell: that is, our inability to fathom the mind and the power and the love of the Trinity. God is telling us to accept in faith that all things will be well and that, in the end, we will see this with joy. God is telling us this for our comfort.

Julian follows this with her extraordinary observation that, on the last day, the Blessed Trinity will posit an act. She knows not what it is or how it will be done, only God knows, but once it is performed all manner of things will be well and, only at that time, will we see it for ourselves. In his wisdom he wants to conceal it from us right now and he wants us to be at peace and ease about it.

God has known this deed, whatever it is, from the beginning. From all eternity, God had intended to make all things well. There may even be an allusion here to chapter 1 of Genesis where God saw that all he made was good. Julian then considers one article of faith that, like all articles of faith, is based on God's word: namely, that hell is real. There are condemned souls as well as condemned angels in hell. This is the clear teaching of Holy Church. How then, is it possible for all things to be well? As our Lord emphasizes, so Julian insists that she is called to maintain firmly what the Church teaches and also to believe, as the Lord has told her, that all things will be well. She accepts the contradiction by simply stating that, for the Lord, nothing is impossible. Systematic logic is not where Julian is at this moment! It is a moment of faith: the substance of things that appear not.

Once again Julian states, at the end of this chapter, her certain belief that what the Church teaches is true and what God says is the same truth—even though, for us, this is impossible to reconcile. This great and secret deed that the Trinity will perform on the Day of Judgment will make well all that is not well. According to Julian, the only human being who knows what this act will be is Christ.

Are we applying too much systematic logic to say that the secret act is going to bring about a great change in what we know as the divine economy of salvation as the Church teaches it? It is an act: that is, something that God will do that will bring about a change in things as we understand them. It will bring to pass a reality that does not presently exist. It will make all manner of things well! We shall see it for ourselves. Julian avoids saying that hell will be eliminated because that seems contrary to Church teaching. She is saying that the existence of hell prevents all manner of things from being well. Her conclusion? Be at peace, have faith in God, and you will see for yourself.

♨

33

MORE ON FAITH

In the context of this vision, Julian desires to learn something more of hell and purgatory. This is not given to her. She asks the reader to recall that in her fifth revelation she saw the devil endlessly condemned. She took this to mean that all of the devil's followers were also condemned, whether they were baptized or not. The vision was one of goodness with little mention of evil. She reminds us that, in three of her visions so far, she has seen the passion of Christ and the sufferings of our Lady and of Christ's true friends. She has not seen anything regarding those who put him to death, but she knows by her faith that they have been damned, unless they were converted by grace.

Once again, Julian refers back to the deed that God will posit on the Day of Judgment. We should try to let it go and desire, like our brethren in heaven, only that God's will be done. The more we strive to know God's secrets, the less knowledge we will have of them. Is Julian, here and in the next chapter protesting too much? Is she wary of the Holy Office of the Inquisition, which was all too busy persecuting heresy in England at the time?

∅

34

TWO MYSTERIES

There are difficulties in understanding this chapter. God has shown Julian two mysteries: one is the great mystery that she has been talking about and that will be hidden until the end of time; the other contains the mysteries God wishes to make known to us. Our blindness and our ignorance have caused them to be hidden from us. Because of this, God has great pity and he wishes to reveal them to us so that we may know, love, and cling to him. He will graciously show us all that we need to understand.

God is actually doing this in this revelation and in the teaching of Holy Church. God is pleased with all men and women who humbly accept the teachings of Holy Church. God is his Holy Church: its ground and substance, teaching and end. In her third revelation, Julian saw that God does everything that is done and, in this doing, she saw no sin. And then God told her that all is well. Later, when God showed her sin, he spoke of the future and said that all shall be well.

∅

35

THE BEST OF ALL POSSIBLE WORLDS

At this stage of the revelations and aware of God's great goodness, Julian decides to ask God about the welfare of a certain friend. She refers to this friend as a creature, no doubt, to avoid getting too personal. God does not respond to this request, but rather, Julian is given an interior locution that tells her that it is better to see God's love and mercy in all things than to focus on one given individual thing. There is more joy in beholding God in everything than in only one thing. By his Trinitarian power, wisdom, and love, God has created all things and so he directs all things.

God looks on everything that he has done as righteous; it cannot be improved upon. He views evil with an honorable toleration because of his mercy and grace, which will last as long as sin is allowed to pursue righteous souls. We fall by his honorable toleration; we are preserved by his love, power, and wisdom; and our joy is increased by his mercy and grace. Like most other mystics, Julian is convinced that we live in the best of all possible worlds.

36

ANOTHER DEED

The beginning of this chapter can only be understood by reading the full chapter. Even then, there are some problems. Julian talks about another deed that the Lord will perform. It is not the great, secret deed she has previously spoken about, which will only be known on the Day of Judgment. It is another that will be done by the Lord with respect to Julian and her fellow Christians.

They will do nothing but sin; but their sin will not impede the Lord's goodness. We are given to understand that this new deed will be performed out of the Lord's mercy precisely because we have sinned. It will be honorable, wonderful, and plentiful with respect to all of those who will be saved; we shall be greatly comforted by it.

The act seems to have some relationship to our reflections on those who are damned, but will have specific reference to our own bliss. Possibly, it is the deed Julian refers to in chapter 42. We are told to be comforted and to rejoice in our salvation. The Lord knows what he is doing and it should not be a matter of concern for us. Perhaps that is the meaning of this second deed: Take comfort and joy in whatever the Lord does, even if it seems to be distressful. This is our role; for we do have a place in it. The first secret deed, however, is something that the Lord will do on his own regarding the economy of salvation. We will know it only after the Day of Judgment.

Julian ends this chapter with what seems to be a digression, a special revelation about miracles. Before miracles happen, we usually experience sorrow and anguish because we need to know our own weaknesses and be humbled and cry to God for help. The Trinity responds to this in power, wisdom, and goodness, and reveals to us, even in this life, something of the joys of heaven through his miracles. The ultimate purpose of miracles is that we might grow in faith and hope. Is a miracle to be expected in reference to this second deed?

&

37

SIN AND THE GODLY

While Julian was lost in the delight of beholding God, he gently and patiently reminded her that she would sin. She saw that this referred not only to herself, but to all her fellow Christians. The Lord assured them that they would sin but also lovingly promised them his protection. God loves all who will be saved and this causes Julian herself to love them all the more.

Julian frequently uses the expression "all who will be saved." At first glance, one might think she speaks this way because she is very conscious of those who will *not* be saved. This is not the case. Julian wishes to avoid any indication that she is excluding some people because they are condemned. She is concerned only with salvation and not with condemnation, as the Lord has gently advised her. There is a higher part of the soul that never sins, because it has a godly will that shall never choose evil. This seems to correspond roughly with what *The Cloud* expresses as a fundamental option for the good. Such a soul never sins mortally. The Lord tells Julian that he loves us here on earth as well as he will love us in heaven. We suffer here only because love is lacking on our side.

∅

38

FROM SIN TO GLORY

Julian's treatment of sin in this chapter is extraordinary. Sin, she says, will not bring shame to a Christian, but honor. Just as there is a corresponding pain for every sin, so there is a corresponding honor for that sin as it is overcome. One thinks of Mary

Magdalene, whom Julian singles out, and of whom it was said that much was forgiven her because she loved much. Julian also mentions St. John of Beverly, apparently a local saint whose legend has been forgotten. Julian tells us that he had fallen into sin but was protected by God so that he died in his grace. Miracles at his tomb were anticipated, as Julian instructs us in chapter 36, by the sufferings in his life that preceded those miracles.

꧁

39

DO NOT DESPAIR

Sin is a scourge so harsh that it often convinces the sinner that he is fit only for hell. The grace of the Holy Spirit must make him contrite and turn his bitterness into hope. The sinner then confesses his sins according to the commands of the Church and performs a suitable penance. He also humbly accepts any bodily ailments sent by God, along with contempt of the world and all kinds of affliction and temptations.

The Lord protects us with his loving care and because our meekness raises us up very high in his sight. He visits us with contrition, compassion, and longing for him so that we become equal with the saints. We are prepared by compassion, made clean by contrition, and made worthy by longing for God. All sinners who will be saved are healed in this way and God sees their wounds as honors. Because of his love he assigns no blame, and shame will be turned into joy. Even those who sin often and grievously need not despair, because their falling does not hinder God's love. Even though we are not always in peace and love, peace and love are always working in us.

꧁

40

GOD LOVES US EVEN IN SIN

God is our great friend and protects us even while we are in sin. He makes us aware of our sins, and we then imagine that he is angry with us. However, the Holy Spirit guides us by contrition to prayer and the desire for amendment until our conscience is at rest and our hope for forgiveness is a reality. Then God joyfully shows himself to us with a friendly greeting. He has always been with us in our suffering and now we see his love and are united to him in bliss. It is the working of the Holy Spirit and the power of Christ's Passion that keeps us safe in peace and love. Whatever may be lacking in this life is supplied for by our prayer and longing for God.

Julian cautions the reader not to misunderstand the Lord's teaching that he brings honor from sin. To say that it is good to sin and thus to receive the Lord's mercy and honor is to be led by folly. True love teaches us to hate sin and to prefer any pain in preference to it. Indeed, sin is the only real pain that afflicts the soul. It is God's power and wisdom and the teachings of Christ that save us. We can see that God is love and that he desires us to be like him in that love, in union with our fellow Christians. Just as his love for us is not destroyed by our sin, so we should never allow our love for one another to be destroyed. God offers us endless comfort by saying that he will keep us full safely.

☙

Sin is necessary! God does not judge.
God is Love.

41

THE FOURTEENTH REVELATION

The next three chapters are extremely beautiful and encouraging. They tell us of the spiritual locutions that Julian received from the Lord regarding prayer. They deserve a special place in the hearts of all who seek the Lord in prayer. The Lord revealed to Julian two conditions that should be present in prayer: prayer should involve confident trust and it should be done correctly. Often our trust is not confident because we think that God does not hear us due to our own unworthiness, and also because of barrenness and dryness, we feel nothing at all.

The Lord tells us that he himself is the source of all our prayer. It is his will that we should have what we ask for in rightful prayer. He makes us wish it, and then he makes us ask for it. How then could it be that we would not receive what we ask for? God is delighted to give us what we ask for. It is impossible that we should seek mercy and grace and not receive it. This is what correct prayer is directed toward. Whatever Our Lord inspires us to ask for, he has ordained from all eternity. So our asking is not actually the cause of the grace he gives us, but it is his own goodness that causes it. This is what God means by telling us that he is the source of all our prayer. This should be for us a great source of encouragement.

When we pray, the Holy Spirit unites us to the Lord's will in a gracious and permanent state of the soul. Julian here uses an illusion to the scriptural passage about having treasure in heaven. Jesus receives our prayer with gratitude and joy and places it in a heavenly treasure house where it will never perish and where it constantly intercedes before God and his saints. Our prayer takes on a life of its own, a life that is not separate from the Lord's. It is the Lord's blessed will that we should pray. He expects it and wants it, for it makes us like to himself. This is why God makes clear in the next revelation that we will have him for our reward. Even though we may not feel it, we should pray with our whole heart. Our prayer is most pleasing to him when it comes from dryness, barrenness, and weakness. It is the Lord who gives life, power, and efficacy to our prayer.

Thanksgiving is an important part of our prayer. With true awareness and great reverence, we turn ourselves joyfully to the activity the Lord guides us to. Sometimes, our thanksgiving breaks out in prayer with a joyful voice, and other times we are dry and feel nothing. However, the heart is driven by common sense and grace to call upon the Lord with our voices. The power of our Lord's word enters the soul, enlivens the heart, and causes it to pray most blessedly and truly to the delight of the Lord.

☙

42

HOW WE SHOULD PRAY

There are three things that our Lord wants us to know about prayer. He wants us to know that he is the ground of our prayer and it is his will. Our manner of performing our prayer is to turn our will into his will. And finally, the fruit of our prayer is to be united with the Lord in all things. Our prayer should be as generous as our trust, in order to pay full homage to the Lord. If we do not do this, it is only because we do not truly understand that our prayer proceeds from him and that it is given by grace from his love.

Julian takes for granted that we understand that all prayer is directed toward asking for mercy and grace. We cannot ask for mercy and grace unless we have already received it. Sometimes, we think that we have prayed for a long time and we do not have what we asked for. This is only because the Lord is waiting for a better occasion in which to bless us more abundantly.

The Lord wants us to know three further things. The first is our noble creation; the second is our precious redemption; and the third is that everything else was made to serve us. We are reminded here of the beautiful statement from *The Cloud* that we were made to love and everything else was made to make love possible. It seems that Julian now makes reference to the second deed that the Lord will do for us (cf. chapter 36). In fact, it is already being done: he is ruling and guiding us in this life to bring us his bliss. Having done this, he has done everything. When we pray, we should understand this.

It is with true longing and trust that we should understand the fullness of joy to come. We long because we savor the bliss to which we are destined. We trust because we truly understand and love our Savior who graces us with this trust. Our Lord does not demand of us anything less than what we are obliged to do. When we humbly beseech him for mercy and grace, we shall find in him everything lacking in us. Again, this is what God meant when he said that he is the source of all our prayer.

�❧

43

CONTEMPLATIVE PRAYER

The soul, created in the image of God, lost that image by sin, but it was restored by grace. Even so, because of individual sins, the soul is often unlike God in condition. Prayer unites the soul to God. It is a witness that the soul wills what God wills. It also gives us peace of mind. So God teaches us to pray, trusting that he will answer the prayer, because he loves us and wants us to be partners in his good work. He gives us the grace to pray that his will be done and that he will do what is pleasing to him. In this way the soul is of one accord with God.

Julian goes on to speak of prayer specifically in the contemplative dimension. When, by a special grace, the Lords shows himself to our soul, we have everything we could desire. We are given over completely to gazing upon him. This is the contemplative experience. Julian calls this prayer exalted and imperceptible and says that it is so delightful that we can no longer pray except as the Lord moves us. This is not the same as seeing the Lord face to face as we will in heaven. But it is a special grace in which the Lord gives us a kind of super strength to share himself here on earth.

The more the soul sees of God by grace, the more she prays to see him even better. But when we do not see him, we then feel the need to pray. So whether we see him or do not see him, the Lord is driving us by his love and it is the time for prayer. When she says that we see the Lord, Julian is speaking of contemplation in the *via positiva*. It is a kind of gazing on the Lord, but only an imperfect one. Nonetheless, it is different from the *via negativa*, such as embraced by *The Cloud*, where one only sees the absence of God in a mystical darkness.

Julian does touch upon the negative way, as all mystics must, when she says that God's wonderful goodness fills our powers so divinely that it surpasses all our imagining and everything we can understand or think. Again, in the positive approach, Julian speaks of coming into the Lord now by secret touchings and spiritual sights, given by the Holy Spirit to the degree that we can bear it. This means they are limited, and it is only after we die that we shall come into the Lord with the fullness of all our spiritual senses activated. We will truly see him, completely feel him, spiritually hear him, delectably smell him, and sweetly taste him. Only then will we see God face to face.

⌀

44

TRUTH, WISDOM, AND LOVE

Julian feels free to hearken back to previous revelations to elucidate her present ones. Her first vision especially has a dynamic connection to all the others. In all the revelations, she says, God showed that humankind does his will and works for his glory continuously. In the first revelation, this was shown to be so in the soul of our Lady, who acted in truth and wisdom by the grace of the Holy Spirit. Truth sees God, who is endless truth; wisdom contemplates God, who is supreme wisdom; and from these two comes endless, supreme, uncreated love, which is God.

Our souls also reflect this wisdom, truth, and love from their creation. They always do what they were created for. They see, contemplate, and love God. So God rejoices in the creature and the creature rejoices in God and sees God, his maker, who is so great in comparison with himself, the creature, that he is brought to perfect humility. There is now nothing left to interfere with his seeing and knowing the truth and wisdom of God and his consequent realization that he is made for eternal love.

☙

45

TWO JUDGMENTS

— God's love
— The Church, Reconciled in Chap. 51

Julian saw herself (and her fellow Christians) subject to two judgments. The first judgment was from God and proceeded from his endless love. In this, Julian saw him assign no blame to us. She received no comfort from this because there was another judgment, that of the Church, which was constantly before her. By this judgment she had to recognize herself as a sinner sometimes deserving of blame and wrath. She did not see these in God's higher judgment given to her in her revelations. She had to accept this higher judgment. But at the same time, the lower judgment of blame and wrath had been given to her previously by the Church, and therefore she could not ignore it.

Julian desired greatly to see in God in what way the lower judgment of the Church was true in his sight so that both judgments might be reconciled. (The only answer she was given is found in chapter 51 in the story of a lord and his servant.) All heavenly things and all earthly things that belong to heaven are contained in these two judgments. The Holy Spirit's guidance in regard to these two judgments gives us knowledge and understanding, and this, in turn, leads us to know our failures. The more we understand our failures, the more grace will prompt us to long for and be filled with endless bliss. Julian is again repeating a basic spiritual maxim found in all mystics: knowledge of self is foundational to knowledge of God. Knowledge of self and humility (understanding our failures) allow the Holy Spirit to fill us with his presence without the interference of our false self.

✑

46

KNOWING OURSELVES

Julian continues to stress that we must come to know ourselves truly and clearly in order to know the Lord truly and clearly. We will never, however, know ourselves completely until the moment of death. It is in our nature and given to us also by grace to desire with all our power to know ourselves in order to know God.

Julian takes up again the conundrum of the two opposing revelations: God imputes to us no blame, but the Church says we are sinners and deserving of suffering and wrath. Despite all this, Julian insists that in her revelations she saw that the Lord was never angry and never will be, because he is good; he is truth, love, and peace, and his power, wisdom, and charity will never allow him to be angry. It is against God's nature to be angry; it is contrary to his goodness. Between God and our soul there is neither wrath nor forgiveness. Our souls are so wholly united to God because of his goodness and love that nothing can interpose between God and our souls.

God has given Julian this understanding in every revelation. He wishes us to know how this is so insofar as it is appropriate for us. At the same time, God tells Julian that there are many hidden mysteries that will only be known at the time when God makes us worthy of them. Julian is satisfied with this and waits upon the Lord to manifest his will. Meanwhile she submits herself to holy mother Church, as a simple child should.

ℴ

47

THE CAUSE OF SIN

The soul owes it to God that we wonder at him in reverence and that we suffer meekly, always rejoicing in him. God wants us to know that we will soon see clearly in him all that we desire. Julian had been taught by Holy Church that the mercy and forgiveness of God consist in a remission of his anger should we sin. She accepts this even though it is never shown to her to be so in her revelations. We shall soon see that the anger was never in God but in ourselves.

And this is what Julian understands. In this life, through simplicity and ignorance, humankind falls into sin. He is weak and foolish and his will is overpowered when he is stressed. Actually, because he does not see God, he is blinded; if he saw God continually, he would never even be tempted to sin. This seems to Julian to be more noble and gracious than what she has previously been taught. But even more noble and gracious is the great desire that the soul has to see God.

Julian feels in herself five kinds of activity: rejoicing, because she has seen God; mourning, because of personal weakness; desire, because she can never rest until she sees him clearly in heaven; fear, that she might be left on her own; and hope, because she sees she will be brought to bliss. Because she rejoices in this hope, the mourning and fear are not very painful. She realizes that we do not persist in this understanding throughout our lifetime, so we fail to perceive God and we fall back upon ourselves. This happens because of original sin and we are burdened and tempted with the feelings of sin and of pain.

⌾

48

MERCY AND GRACE ARE THE ANSWERS

In this chapter, Julian begins to resolve the discrepancies between her visionary experience of the mercy of God and the Church's teaching on his justice. The Holy Spirit dwells in our soul, protects us, gives us peace through grace and reconciles us to God. This is God's mercy and this is how he guides us through the vagaries of our life. The only anger that Julian sees is on humankind's side. Anger is perverse and the opposite of peace and love. It comes from a lack of power, wisdom, or goodness.

This lack is not found in God but it is found in human beings. Through sin, we have in us anger and a continuing opposition to peace and love. This is why God looks upon us with compassion and pity. The foundation of mercy is in love, and the operation of mercy is to give protection in love.

Mercy is sweet, gracious, and loving. It works to protect us and turns everything to good for us. It even allows us to fail to a certain extent. To the degree that we fail, we fall; and to the degree that we fall, we die. To the extent that we fail to see and experience God who is our life, to that extent, we die. Our failing, falling, and dying are dreadful, shameful, and sorrowful. But in all this, God looks on us with pity and his mercy does not end.

Mercy has the quality of compassion that belongs to motherhood. (Julian here anticipates her understanding of the motherhood of God.) Grace has the quality of dominion that belongs to a king. Mercy protects, gives life, and provides healing in all the tenderness of love. Grace works with mercy—raising, rewarding, and exceeding all we deserve. It displays the vast generosity of God's royal power and his wonderful graciousness. This transforms our failing into unending solace, our shameful falling into an honorable rising, and our sorrowful dying into a blessed life.

Our sinfulness here on earth gives us pain, shame, and sorrow. Grace, when we are in heaven, gives us such great solace, honor, and bliss that we shall bless the Lord that we ever suffered woe because, without it, we could never know the blessed love that God has for us. When Julian sees all of this, she is forced to agree that the mercy of God and his forgiveness dispels our anger.

❧

49

GROUNDED IN PEACE

It is a great marvel to observe in everything, time and time again, that the Lord in himself cannot forgive because he cannot be angry. Our life is grounded in love and without love we cannot survive. The soul recognizes that we are endlessly made one with God in love and that it is the most impossible thing in the world for God to be angry at us. God who destroys our anger and makes us meek is himself meek in love, which is the opposite of anger. God makes us his friends, and anger and friendship cannot exist together.

Julian sees no kind of wrath in God. If God could be angry for even an instant we should have neither life nor being. We have our being and our preservation from the power, wisdom, and endless goodness of God. Anger would be contrary to this. We may feel in ourselves anger and strife, but we are all mercifully enveloped in God's meekness and goodness.

Julian observes clearly that our friendship, life, and being are in God. That same goodness that protects us from perishing when we sin, constantly summons us into peace—opposing our anger and making us recognize our fearful need to beg God for forgiveness. Our salvation requires that we be truly in peace and love, without anger.

Our evil propensities may cause us to be angry and in distress; still we are saved by God's merciful care. We are not, however, blessedly safe and in possession of eternal joy until we are in peace and in love with all of God's works and judgments. Moreover, we must be loving and content with ourselves, our fellow Christians, and everything that God loves. It is God and his goodness that bring this about in us.

When we are disquieted, God is our true peace. By the operation of mercy and grace he makes us meek, which, in turn, makes us completely safe. When the soul is united to God, she is truly at peace within herself, because in God is found no wrath. Contrariness is the cause of our woe and the Lord Jesus takes it up to heaven and makes it sweeter than we can think or say. In heaven we shall find our tribulations and our woes turned into true beauty and honor.

⌀

50

CONTINUED PERPLEXITY

According to the judgment of men, we are often spiritually dead by reason of the trials and the grief we fall into. Yet, as God sees it, the soul destined for salvation never was and never shall be dead. Julian wonders greatly at the problem this presents. God is truth itself and she knows in truth that we often sin seriously and are blameworthy. Yet she also knows another truth: namely, she never sees God showing us any kind of blame. How can this be so?

Julian understands from the teaching of the Church and through her own personal experience that the blame for our sins hangs continuously upon us. Thus it is a matter of great wonder to her that she never sees God show us any more blame than if we were as pure as the angels in heaven.

Her reasoning in this matter was challenged by her blindness. She needed to know how God looks upon us in our sins. She felt that she should either see in God that sin was done away with, or else she should see in God how he views it, so she could properly understand sin and blame. Her thinking went this way: If I should understand that we are not sinners or blameworthy, it seems that

I would be in error; but if I should understand that we are sinners and blameworthy, how is it that, because of my revelations, I cannot see that as true? For Julian, this was a very basic issue that she needed to understand so she might be able to discern good and evil. Reason and grace would then help her to separate one from another so she would love God and hate evil as the Church teaches.

☙

5 1

THE LORD AND THE SERVANT

This is the longest and, many would say, the most important chapter in Julian's book. If one reads carefully Julian's explanation of the development of her understanding of this revelation, it need not be as complicated as first seems. We must understand that Julian is really telling a new story but, at the same time, repeating mysteries or, if you will, secrets contained in the teachings of the Church. We must not confuse her parable of the Lord and the servant with the account in Genesis of the fall of Adam. It is not unrelated to this, but neither is it a simple repetition. It is something new and refreshing. One might even say, with careful reservations, that it is the fall of Adam without original sin or, at any rate, without original sin as we traditionally see it, involving guilt and blame. It concerns the New Adam, who was free from any stain of sin while still bearing the burden of sin. Julian does not once quote the scripture directly in this chapter, but it is replete with scriptural allusions. She leaves it up to the reader to recognize them.

The Lord answers Julian's question from the previous chapter by revealing to her the example of a Lord and his servant. It is a very simple story with bodily visions of both the Lord and the servant and also with a spiritual understanding of them. The Lord is sitting quite peacefully in state; the servant is standing beside him ready to do his bidding. The Lord lovingly sends him on an errand. The servant, because of his love, dashes off with great speed to do his Lord's will. In his haste, the servant almost immediately falls into a ditch. He is badly injured and groans and tosses about, unable to help himself in any way. Although he is not far away from his Lord, his greatest grief is that he is not able even to turn in his direction and see him, as it were, for consolation. In his weakness and folly, he is much concerned with his own distressful condition.

Julian says the servant suffers seven great pains—seven being a mystical number and referring to the complete gamut of possible agonies. Anticipating further development in this revelation, it would be helpful to see these pains as the afflictions Adam and all men and women suffered from Adam's fall, as well as the pains that Jesus suffered as a result of his Incarnation and especially in his Passion. The severe bruising from the servant's fall, the clumsiness and weakness of his body, his mental confusion about his love for the Lord, his inability to rise, his total loneliness, and the wretchedness of the place where he was trapped—all these cause the servant great pain.

Julian is amazed that the servant could so meekly accept all this suffering. She looks carefully to see if she can detect any fault in him or if the Lord is imputing to him any blame. But truly she can see neither fault nor blame. Here is where Julian significantly departs from the traditional account of Adam's fall being the result of sin. She draws the line between what she has been taught by the Church and what her revelations teach her. This is the paradox she attempts to resolve in this chapter as a faithful daughter of the Church and a docile recipient of her revelations. She states that the only reason the servant fell was his eager desire to do his Lord's

will. She does not see it as a sin of pride or a willful submission to
Satan's temptations.

All this time, Julian observes that the Lord looks upon his servant lovingly, with great compassion and at the same time great
joy over the rewards he is planning to bestow upon him. In her
heart, Julian hears the Lord praise his servant because of the injuries he has received in his service. Should he not reward the servant because of his fright, injuries, and all his sufferings? Should
he not even give him a gift that would be more honorable than
his own health would have been had he not fallen? Does not the
Lord's own honor require that his beloved servant should be highly
rewarded so that his falling and all the suffering resulting from it
would be turned into high honor and endless happiness?

Even without further explanations from Julian, the mind of the
reader reels from the implications of these statements. Are they not
already responding to the difficult observation that sin is necessary
and that forgiveness is not needed? This is only the beginning of
the resolution of this conflict. Julian recognizes this but is not yet
comforted because she cannot understand it fully. Clearly, there is
more to come.

Part of the problem for Julian is that she recognizes that the servant has been shown to her as representing Adam, and yet she sees
in him a number of characteristics that could not be attributed to
Adam. This, as we shall see, is because the servant is also a symbol for Christ. At the point of the revelation, Julian realized that
this mystery was only gradually being unfolded for her, and that
the Lord would make it clear to her when he so willed it. In fact,
it took twenty years! During this time, Julian was told to reflect
with great care on all the details of this example of the Lord and
his servant. She then proceeds to do this.

Julian is given to understand that the Lord who sat in state and
peace is God. The servant who stood there is Adam, and his fall

was seen as the fall of every man and woman, so we could realize how God regards all of us, and all our falls. In the sight of God all humankind is one man. This man fell, was injured in his faculties, and made feeble in his physical powers. Thus, he was unable to look upon his Lord. His good will, however, was preserved in the Lord's sight. Because he was wounded in his faculties, the man was hindered from realizing that the Lord approved and commended him for his good will. So the man could neither look upon his Lord nor understand how the Lord, in his compassion, looked upon him with such love. Julian understands that when we can truly and wisely look upon the Lord, we can realize his love and compassion. Then we shall be at rest and at peace here on earth, in part, and in heaven, in its fullness.

Julian recognizes this as the beginning of a real understanding of her problem: that is, precisely how does God look upon us in our sin? She realizes that the gracious God offers comfort and help and lovingly desires to bring us happiness. At the same time she understands, as she said before, that evil has no metaphysical being, but that pain is very real. It is pain, the fruit of sin, that blames and punishes, not the Lord.

Julian now returns to a detailed consideration of her vision. The Lord sits in a lonely, deserted, and empty wasteland. His clothing, as befitting a Lord, is ample, handsome, colorful, and dignified. His eyes and his countenance are dark but beautiful, and reveal all his love and compassion. One can see within him a place of secure refuge. The loving regard that he focuses on his servant, especially when he falls, would melt the heart for love and break it in two for joy. His loving regard contains an earthly pity and a heavenly bliss.

Julian now, for the first time, explicitly refers to the servant as Our Lord Jesus Christ, as well as Adam. As will be necessary in the circumstances, she distinguishes between the two, and in other circumstances she speaks of them as being identical. This, of course, is justified because of the Incarnation, when the Lord Jesus Christ took upon himself our human, Adamic flesh. The Father's earthly pity was for Adam, his most beloved creature, while his heavenly bliss was for the falling of his beloved Son, who was equal to the Father in all things. The falling of God the Son was from his place in the Trinity down into the Virgin's womb, whence he would experience all the sufferings of humanity. This was the same as the fall of the servant into the ditch. The Father's mercy and pity filled all the earth, accompanied Adam into hell (not the hell of the damned but the "limbo" where Adam awaited his redemption in Christ), kept him and all humankind from endless death, and remains with him until he is received in heaven.

Humankind is blind in this life and cannot see the Father. So the Father presents himself in a familiar way. This is why he shows himself sitting in a barren and wasted place. His preference is to dwell in humankind's soul, God's true city; but when the servant falls into sorrow and pain it is not proper for him to serve in that high office. Instead of preparing some other place, the Father simply sits on the ground while he waited for human nature (which is made partly from the earth) to be restored by his beloved Son to its noble place of beauty. Julian greatly rejoices when she sees this honorable restoration, which the Father wants to bring about for his servant by his plentiful grace.

The father is sitting in state. By this, Julian wishes to indicate that he is impassive, possessing all perfection and therefore totally incapable of change. The servant is standing before his Lord (or rather, to one side, as we shall see), clothed like a laborer whose white tunic is old, scanty, and worn. It is stained with sweat, tight fitting, short, threadbare, and about to fall into rags. It is a symbol of his humanity. Julian is surprised to see a servant so greatly beloved standing before such a gracious Lord in this kind of clothing. She is given the realization that, in spite of his outward appearance, internally the servant loves the Lord as much as the Lord loves him.

The servant wisely understands that he could best pay homage to the Lord if he had no regard for himself or anything that might happen to him. So he goes off in great haste when his Lord sends him to do something. This is to his credit for it is evident by his clothing that he has been a constant laborer and is now newly appointed to the service of his Lord.

Julian speaks strangely of a treasure in the earth that the Lord loves. She is given to understand that it is a special food. There are allusions here to the Genesis description of Adam being consigned to till the earth and care for it. Julian sees that the servant has been sent to perform some very difficult work as a gardener. He is to dig and sweat and turn the soil over and over and to keep the plants watered. He is to keep at this work until it has produced some fine fruit to bring before his master for his delight, prepared exactly as he likes it. Meanwhile, his Lord is sitting in the same place waiting for the return of his servant.

Julian wonders where the servant has come from. She sees that the Lord has within himself endless life and every kind of goodness except for that treasure which is in the earth and that is grounded in the depth of his endless love. She does not understand completely what all this means.

The servant is the Second Person of the Trinity and, at the same time, Adam, who signifies all men and women. The Son is the Godhead equal to the Father; the servant is the humanity of the Son who is the true Adam. The servant, the Divine Son, stands near his Lord; but the servant, as Adam, stands to his left side. The Lord is the Father, God. The servant is the Son, Christ Jesus. The Holy Spirit, of course, is also present as the love they have for one another.

When Adam fell, so did the Son of God, because they are one. The Son of God could not be separated from Adam—that is, from all men and women. Adam fell from life to death into the ditch of this wretched world, while the Son of God fell with Adam but into the womb of our Lady, so he might bring salvation to Adam. In all this, Julian understands that the Son of God and Adam are but one man, who is everyone, and whose virtue and goodness are from Christ, while his weakness and blindness are from Adam.

Here now is the key and the heart of Julian's understanding of the problem she has been confronting. The Lord Jesus takes upon himself all our blame and, therefore, the Father cannot assign to us more blame than he does to his beloved Son. This is why Julian sees no blame coming from the Father upon the servant. Christ also is the servant standing before the Father from all eternity until the fullness of time, when he rushed off to perform his Father's bidding and perform that mission that would bring all humankind back to heaven. Thus, he fell into the ditch—that is into our humanity—and, by doing this, accomplished his Father's will. This is why the Father could not assign to him guilt or blame. When the father looked upon the servant in agony, trapped in the ditch, he saw his own beloved Son in whom he is well pleased. His beloved Son bore humankind's pain and suffering, and by his wounds we were healed. There is no place in this scenario for forgiveness, guilt, or blame. There is only the compassionate look of the Father, joyfully anticipating the glory to which he would bring the Son, and with him all the human race.

This marvelous example provides Julian with an understanding of the very fundamentals of salvation. All humankind will be saved by the sweet Incarnation and Passion of Christ. Christ is the head and we are the members of the body. The day will come, as yet unknown to us, when every tear will be taken away and everlasting joy will be given us. Everyone in heaven longs to see this and we, who are under heaven, will come there by having that same desire and longing as was shown in the servant, Christ in

Adam's tunic, standing before the Lord. In Jesus is the desire and longing of all humankind who will be saved.

The servant is shown standing to the left of the Father rather than seated equally with him because the Son of God, in his role as the new Adam, had to undergo the labor of suffering all humanity's pain in his passion and death. It was only when he handed his soul over to his Father that he was able to display his power. He then descended into hell (not the hell of the damned) to bring back with him the root of Jesse, that is, the remnant of the faithful who were awaiting their salvation through his death and resurrection. And so the writhing and the groaning and the suffering of the fall were ended. The feeble, mortal flesh that Christ took upon himself as Adam's tunic was made lovely, new, bright, and forever wide, ample, and fair.

Julian concludes this chapter with a new vision that is a full and complete statement of God's work of salvation. No longer does the Father sit on the ground in the wilderness but on a heavenly throne. No longer does the Son stand before the Father as a servant, but rather sits at his right hand in endless rest and peace, wearing a precious crown, which consists of the souls of all who will be saved. We are his crown, which is the Father's joy, the Son's honor, and the Holy Spirit's delight.

$\mathscr{B}$

52

GOD IS WITH US

As Jesus is all things to all men and women, so is the Trinity. It would seem that Julian was raised in a healthy, functional family. The ease with which she identifies the relationships of the Trinity in a family context seems to indicate this. She saw that God rejoices that he is our Father, our Mother, and our true spouse. Christ rejoices that he is our brother and Jesus rejoices that he is our savior. Theologically, the name of Christ is given to the Son of God after the Resurrection, while the name of Jesus belongs to him from the Incarnation until his death.

All of us have, in our lives on earth, alternating periods of well-being and woe. This is because we have in us the risen Lord as well as the fallen Adam. We are protected by the risen Christ and fragmented by Adam's falling. The various pains, sins, and blindnesses we receive from Adam discomfort us. Nonetheless, God works in us to await his mercy and grace. We are given, in his goodness, greater or lesser insights to understand this. We rise and then we fall again into our blindness and sorrows. The one constant in all this, however, is our intention to be with God with all our heart, soul, and strength. But still, when the joy of this is hidden, we fall again into blindness.

We are comforted when our faith assures us that, by the strength of Christ, we never consent to serious sin. Christ wills that we should trust in his presence with us in three ways: he is with us in heaven, calling us to himself; he is with us on earth, leading us; he is present in our souls, caring for us.

We saw in the servant the misfortunes of Adam and also the goodness of God's Son. We also saw compassion for Adam's suffering and the endless honor humankind is given by virtue of the

Passion and death of Christ. So the Lord rejoices greatly in Adam's falling because of the noble rising that humankind has come to. It surpasses anything we would have had if Adam had not fallen. So we mourn because our sins, which we hate, caused Christ's pains; and we rejoice because endless love caused him to suffer for us.

Julian comprehends that in our Lord's providence we cannot keep from sin here on earth as totally as we shall in heaven. Grace does protect us from mortal sins and, within reason, helps us avoid venial sins. If, by our blindness, we should fall, we can readily amend ourselves according to the Church's teaching. We can then go forward in love without falling too low or recklessly ignoring our weakness. God's point of view is graciously to forgive humankind while our point of view is humbly to excuse ourselves.

Our Lord wants us to accuse ourselves willingly and recognize our falls and the harms that come from them, as long as we are aware that it is only his everlasting love that reinstates us. We should recognize both of these things. The lower part of a human's life, according to Julian, has two parts. The one is the falling of humankind, while the other is the reparations our Lord has made for us. The strength that we have in the lower part of our life comes from the higher part. The love that brings it about is a double action that touches our sufferings, compassions, forgiveness, and other beneficial things, because of the joy that it gives and the transforming of our guilt into endless honor.

☙

53

GOD ASSIGNS NO BLAME

Julian is given to understand that God never assigns blame to a soul that is to be saved. Such souls never assent to sin. They must be so at one with God that there is preserved in them a godly will that can never be parted from God. This union with God does not do away with the purpose and efficacy of the redemption as Holy Church teaches. God never really began his love affair with humankind; he has known and loved all men and women from the beginning.

Julian alludes here to the first chapter of St. John's Gospel, which tells us that it is through the Second Person of the Trinity, the Word, that all things were made. Christ is the ground, cause, and model of these souls that never consent to sin. Out of him we come, in him we are enclosed, and into him we shall all go and find our complete joy. God loved us before he created us, and when we were created we loved him. This love is created by the goodness of the Holy Spirit, by the power of the Father, and the wisdom of the Son. The human body was created from the slime of the earth, but his soul was made from nothing. And so there can be absolutely nothing that separates God from the human soul.

In God's endless love, the human soul is kept whole. It is led and protected by God and has a life that, by God's grace, shall last for ever in heaven—loving, thanking, and praising him. We were loved by God from the beginning and shall be loved without end. Humankind is the noblest being God ever created and its fullest essence is the soul of Christ. All souls that will be saved are united to God through our creation in the Word and this union makes us holy.

ℬ

54

GOD IN US, WE IN GOD

Where the soul of Christ is, there is the substance of all the souls that God will save. In his endless love, God makes no distinction between the soul of Christ and the least soul to be saved. The dwelling place of our soul is God, and God dwells in our soul. Julian comprehends that there is no difference between God and our essence: our essence is in God; God is God, and our essence is a creature in God. The truth of the Trinity is that it is our Father who made and preserves us and in whom we are enclosed. The wisdom of the Trinity is that it is our Mother within whom we are enclosed. We are wrapped up in the Son also and in the Holy Spirit; but also the Father, the Son and the Holy Spirit are enclosed in us. We receive virtue in our souls by faith, which is given from the Holy Spirit. This virtue consists in a right understanding, true belief, and trust that we are in God and God is in us. This virtue of faith works great things in us and causes us to be living, loving Christians and children of Christ.

⌀

55

CHRIST IS OUR WAY

Christ is our Way. Christ in his risen body contains within himself all of us and he gloriously presents us to his heavenly Father. His Father receives us gratefully and graciously gives us back to his Son. Julian has shown us this very clearly in her ninth revelation (chapter 22). Thus, we are a joy to the Father, bliss to the Son, and a delight to the Holy Spirit. This joy, which is in the Blessed Trinity, gives us joy and gives delight to our Lord.

Our faith comes from the attraction of our soul to God, from our intelligence, and from the stable memory that we have from our creation. No matter whether we are experiencing joy or grief, God wants us to understand that we exist more truly in heaven than on earth.

Mercy and grace have been working in us since we were created, protecting us with pity and love and giving us the hope that we shall return to God in the power of Christ through the Holy Spirit. Our humanity is based on nature, mercy, and grace. This enables us to receive those gifts that lead us to everlasting life. Our essence is in God, and God is in our human nature, which has been destined from all eternity to be the dwelling place of God. All the gifts that God can give us, he has given to his Son, who dwells within us and who, at the same time, encloses us within himself. Our body and our soul cooperate with one another until we have grown into maturity, while the Holy Spirit breathes into us the gifts leading to eternal life.

Our soul is a created trinity, like the uncreated Trinity, loved from the beginning and at the time of creation united to the Creator. These three things—love, mercy, and grace—make us resemble the Trinity. God has made a glorious union between the soul and the body that causes humankind the need to be restored from a double death, that of the soul and that of the body, which could only occur when the Word was made flesh. Julian follows here the teaching of St. Augustine who says that there is in the soul a higher part, always at peace with God, and a lower part, which is our sensuality, our human nature. Christ, in the lower part, suffered for the salvation of humankind. In the higher part, however, he always delights in his divinity.

☙

56

KNOWLEDGE OF THE SOUL

Our soul is so deeply grounded in God that we come more readily to knowing God than to knowing our own soul. So we must know God, in order to know our own soul. This may be a bit confusing because, later in this chapter, Julian will say that we cannot come to a full knowledge of God unless we first know our own soul. Perhaps the operative word is *full* knowledge.

Julian does not contradict herself. Our desire to truly know our own soul comes from our nature, and it is the same as desiring to know God, so close is it to God. Our soul is grounded in God, sits in God in true rest, stands in God in sure strength, and is rooted in God in endless love. It can, therefore, be sought only in God, who is nearer to us than our own soul.

Our essence and our sensuality is in Jesus, who is in repose in the Godhead but who is destined to dwell in our souls forever. In the sixteenth revelation we shall see that Jesus will never be moved from our soul. Jesus already possesses the gifts that the Holy Spirit shall breathe into us and that will lead us to eternal life within us. They are enclosed in him until our souls and bodies are brought by nature to the fullness of their maturity. The power of Christ's passion and the value of our tribulations given us through mercy and grace will bring us to knowledge of our own soul and then to knowledge of God. Julian is once again stating the classic understanding that self-knowledge—humility—is foundational for knowledge of God.

Our reason is grounded in nature, which is grounded in God and from whom mercy and grace spring forth. This is how we have within our souls our own trinity. In our human nature are our life and being, and in mercy and grace are our growth and fulfillment.

To know these three things fully and clearly is to possess the endless joy we shall have in heaven. To be saved, we need mercy and grace as well as our natural origin in God. From these three things acting together, we receive all good things.

Ø

57

HIGHER AND LOWER PARTS

We are created essentially to be so noble that we will always achieve God's will. God loves us and we always do what is pleasing to him. When our soul is incarnated in our body, virtue proceeds from that nobility into our soul. In essence, we are full, but in the flesh we are lacking. God will supply for this lack through mercy and grace, which are given to us from his own goodness. God's natural goodness and the natural goodness that we have from him enable us to receive the operation of mercy and grace.

Our nature is completely in God. In this human nature, God makes various things flow out of him so that we might do his will. The higher part of our human nature is knit to God in creation, and God is knit to the lower part of our human nature by the Incarnation. Our two parts are united in Christ and the Trinity is in him.

Through the revelations, Julian was given to see that all the works God has ever done were completely known to him from the beginning. Out of his love he created humankind and because of the same love he was willing to become a man. By the working of mercy and grace through the natural goodness of God, we receive faith. From faith comes all the other good things that guide us and save us.

From our faith come the commandments of God. We understand that we must love them and keep them and also to hate and refuse what he forbids. In these two things are all our actions contained. Also from our faith come the seven sacraments and all manner of virtues. The virtues that we have received naturally in our human nature through God's goodness are also given to us supernaturally by the action of mercy through the Holy Spirit.

It should be noted here that Julian prefers not to speak of salvation in terms of the sin of Adam and how humankind related to God before and after that sin. Rather she speaks of our essence, our enfleshment, our nobility from God, our natural goodness, our union with the Lord through the Incarnation, and the power of the Holy Spirit working in us through mercy and grace. It seems that Julian prefers not to enter into the mythology of the Garden of Eden. It is evident, however, that the truths of this myth are very much the truths that Julian teaches.

These gifts are treasured for us within Jesus. When he took on our fleshly soul in the Incarnation, he enclosed us all in himself, uniting our fleshly soul to our essence in God. This leads Julian now to recognize how our Lady is our mother. We are all enclosed in her and out of her we are born in Christ. As mother of our Savior, she is mother of all who shall be saved by our Savior. This leads Julian to recognize the motherhood of Jesus in whom we are endlessly born. For Julian, this is neither a sexual nor a feminist issue. The motherhood of Jesus simply proceeds from who he is and what he does. Julian reminds us that this was shown in the first revelation where we are all enclosed in him, and he in us. It will also be spoken of in the sixteenth revelation, where he dwells in our soul. This is his delight. By drawing us to himself, he wishes us to be his helpers, to learn from him, to keep his laws, and to do his will.

‧ℰ‧

58

FATHER, MOTHER, SPOUSE

Julian did not believe in the preexistence of souls. She does speak of our first creation, of our substance, and our essence as being created by the eternal purpose of the Father. God is total perfection and from the very beginning is all that he could possibly be and, from that same beginning, has accomplished all that he could possibly accomplish. In that sense, the substance or essence of souls has existed in him from the very beginning. Also from the beginning has been saved every soul that would be saved. At a certain point in time, there was another creation, a second creation, if you will, in which these souls took on sensual form. It was the work of the Second Person of the Trinity to also take on this sensual form and accomplish, through his Passion and death and Resurrection, our salvation. So we have two parts, a higher part that is our essence and existed in the Father from all eternity, and a lower part that is our sensual form, our second creation, our coming into existence as body/soul human beings. It is the gracious work of the Holy Spirit to unite these two parts in one.

From our first creation, that is in our essence or substance, we are joined and united to the whole Trinity and we are kept as pure and noble as when we were created—that is, from all eternity in the mind of God. By the power of that union, we love our Creator, delight in him, praise him, and endlessly rejoice in him. And so from our very beginning in the heart of God, God is our loving Father by creation. God is our wisdom and our loving Mother; in God is our goodness in the Holy Spirit. In our union with him, he is also our true spouse and we are his beloved wife.

Julian understands the three properties she has seen in the Trinity are: fatherhood, from which we have our protection and bliss in our essence, and our first creation; motherhood, from which we have knowledge and wisdom and the restoration and salvation of our sensuality; and lordship in the Holy Spirit, from which we have the reward we have earned by our labor in cooperation with grace, and the gift that we have been freely given by God's mercy.

From our first creation, in our essence or substance, the high mightiness of the Trinity is our father, the deep wisdom of the Trinity is our mother, and the great love of the Trinity is the Holy Spirit. It is the Second Person of the Trinity who is our mother substantially and also our mother sensually because we are double by God's creation that is, in the upper part, substantial, and in the lower part, sensual. So Jesus is our mother in two senses: in nature through our substantial creation, and in mercy through taking on our sensuality.

In our father, God Almighty, we have our being. In our mother of Mercy we have our restoration, which unites our upper and lower parts into one perfect human. In the Holy Spirit we have our fulfillment. Our substance or essence is in our father, in our mother, and in the Holy Spirit, and it is whole and complete in each person of the Trinity who is one God. Our sensuality, however, is only in the Second Person, Christ Jesus. However, even here we must recognize that in Jesus is the Father and the Holy Spirit.

ଛ

59

TRINITY AND MOTHER

The goodness of mercy and grace that is in God opposes the rising up of wickedness that has been allowed to happen, so that God might turn it into goodness and to the honor of all who will be saved. Julian will soon develop this idea when she speaks of the necessity of sin.

Perhaps more so in this chapter than in any other, Julian concretizes her understanding of the Trinity and of the motherhood of God. For Julian, neither doctrine is an abstract speculation. The foundation of motherhood begins with Jesus Christ, from whom we are born from the first creation and who nurtures us with the protection of his love. God is mother as well as father and reveals this parentage in all that he does. Julian has no problem speaking of God as mother and in the same sentence using the masculine pronoun to refer to God. God is everything a father or mother should be, power and wisdom and grace. All this is in the Trinity, of which God is the unity and the supreme goodness who makes us long for himself and endlessly fulfills that longing.

God has known us and loved us substantially from the beginning. As the Trinity, he desired the Second Person to become the mother, brother, and Savior of our human nature. Just as truly as God is our father so truly is God our mother. As father he wills, as mother he works, and as Holy Spirit he strengthens. So we love God as father in whom we have our being; we pray to him as mother for mercy and pity; and as Holy Spirit we seek help and grace. Once again, Jesus is our true mother in nature by our creation from the beginning, and our true mother in our sensuality. And there is appropriated to him all the sweet offices and the loving works of motherhood. Thus, there are three ways of understanding the motherhood of God. He is the foundation of our very being; he is the incarnation of our nature where he begins the motherhood of grace as son, brother, and Savior; and he is, as the Holy Spirit, motherhood at work.

♨

60

GOD AS MOTHER

Our Lord is our mother in human nature and our mother in grace. He wishes to be our mother in everything. Julian shows here that her twenty-year reflection on her visions is ongoing because she refers back now to her first vision, where she beheld the meekness of our Lady. God, who is supreme wisdom, clothed himself in our flesh in her lowly womb so that he could perform the service of motherhood in everything. The service of a mother is close, because it involves human nature; it is willing, because it is loving; it is certain, because it is true.

Our earthly mothers bring us into a life of pain and dying. But Jesus, our true mother, births us to joy and endless life. He bears us within himself until full-term, suffering the hardest of pains, and gives us birth into bliss. Even this does not satisfy his marvelous love, because, as he tells Julian, if he could suffer more he would do so. Having died for us, he could die no more. Still, he does not cease working for us, but, as behooves motherhood, he still offers us the service of nourishment. He feeds us not with milk, but with himself in the Blessed Sacrament, and indeed, in all the sacraments of Holy Church. Perhaps the reader might feel here that Julian is overdoing the analogy. As a mother lays a child on her breast, our mother, Jesus, leads us into his breast through the wound in his side, and divinely shows us his promise of eternal happiness.

Julian insists that the word "mother," in its fullest sense, can only truly be given to Jesus. To motherhood belong natural love, wisdom, and knowledge. It is not hard to see here an allusion to Ephesians 3:15 and the fatherhood of God from which all fatherhood gets its name. Our physical birth is most humble in comparison with our spiritual birth, but our Lord does even this. He knows and sees our needs as the nature of motherhood requires. And as we grow in age, a mother changes her methods but not her love, even allowing us to be chastised in order to receive mercy and grace. Every obligation that we have to fatherhood and motherhood, by God's command, is truly fulfilled by loving God. It is Christ who works this love in us.

§

61

WE NEED TO FALL

Our Lord brings us to a spiritual birth and then he protects us. He kindles our understanding. He prepares our ways and eases our conscience. He comforts our soul and illuminates our heart. He makes us love everything that he loves for his sake. When we fall, he quickly raises us up. Strengthened by his grace, we willingly choose him forever.

The Lord allows some of us to fall, at times, even more grievously than ever before. Then, because of our lack of wisdom, we think that everything we have undertaken was for nothing. The truth is we need to fall and recognize it or we would not realize how wretched we are by ourselves. Indeed, sin is necessary. Otherwise, we would never know so completely the wonderful love of God. In heaven we shall realize that we have sinned grievously, but we will truly understand that we never lacked God's love or were of less value in his eyes. How great is that love that will not be broken because of offenses!

We shall be raised high in heaven by this profitable understanding of our humility. First we fall, then we recognize it, and both are from God's mercy. A mother can never allow any kind of danger to come to her child because of her love, even though she will allow the child to be distressed in various ways for its own benefit. Our mother Jesus will never allow his children to perish because he manifests the might, wisdom, and love of the Trinity.

When we see our own wretchedness, we become fearful and ashamed of ourselves. Our gracious mother Christ does not wish us to run away, but rather wants us to behave like a child who calls for his mother for help with all its might and quickly runs to her when it is frightened. Christ wants us to plead with him, our gracious and beloved mother, for mercy and help. Our Lord wants us to see that it is profitable for us to mourn and weep. In his compassion and out of his love, he waits until the right time has come. He wants us to show the natural trust a child has in its mother's love in both joy and sorrow. He wants us to find, through faith, our beloved mother in his Holy Church. Any given individual may be broken, but the entire body of Holy Church can never be broken. So it is a good thing to will fervently that we be united to our mother the Church, who is Christ Jesus. Through the Church, our Lord takes on the services of a nurse as well as a mother whose only duty is to care for the welfare of her child. It is his duty and his glory to care for us so that we might love and trust him. And so he keeps us full safely.

ℒ

62

BY NATURE AND BY GRACE

In the revelations, the Lord revealed to Julian all of the frailty, humiliations, and burdens this life offers. But he also revealed his power, wisdom, love, and protection—to his glory and for our salvation. He raises us up to consolation and comfort on high in heaven, and turns everything to his glory and to our joy. This comes from the natural goodness of God through the operation of grace. God has given to humankind all of the natures that he has put separately in different creatures. He is the true father and mother of natures, and they flow out of him to work his will and return to him through their salvation by the operation of grace. Is this, perhaps, an allusion to the Genesis accounts of creation and Adam's role as master of all under God?

We are all united to God by nature and grace. We do not need to search so as to know various natures, but only to go to our mother's breast, which is Holy Church and our own soul where the Lord dwells. Now through faith and understanding, we shall find everything there; afterward, we shall find them through truth, clearly, and in bliss. This is generally true for all human nature, because human nature was prepared for our mother, Christ. This is so that the creation of humanity might be honorable and noble and human salvation might be joyful and blissful.

Julian speaks here of the place humankind has as the summit of God's creation and how all things are brought to salvation through humanity. But the Lord Jesus is the summit of human nature and all things are brought to salvation through him. It is interesting to see how Julian expresses this doctrine without direct reference to scripture or scriptural mythology. Julian is also capable of being left-brained and engaging in some solid metaphysical theology.

✄

63

NATURE SAVED BY GRACE

We hate sin both by nature and by grace. Nature is good in itself and grace is given to save and preserve nature, and to return it to God with even greater nobility and glory. Everyone in heaven will see our nature as tried and tested and found to be without defect. Grace is God and uncreated nature is God. So nature and grace are in accord with one another and work together in love.

When, with God's help, we come to harmony with both our human nature and grace, we shall see sin as it truly is: vile and unnatural. We need not fear this but, in all humility, can express our complaints to Christ our mother, who will restore us with his precious blood to his own honor and our eternal joy. He will continue this work until all his children are saved. Our life is founded in Mother Jesus and in his wisdom from all eternity with the great power of God the Father and the supreme goodness of the Holy Spirit. How frequently Julian brings in the power, wisdom, and goodness of the Trinity!

By becoming flesh, Jesus accepted our nature and, by dying on the cross, he gave birth to us in endless life. Since that time, he cares for us as a loving mother wishes and as the need of childhood requests. Fair is our heavenly mother to our soul, and sweet is our soul to our heavenly mother; mutual is their love! Julian was given to recognize childhood as a stage in life great in weakness and in the lack of strength and intelligence. But when our Mother Jesus returns us to God the Father's glory, then we shall truly understand the meaning of Christ's words that we shall see for ourselves that all manner of things shall be well. And so Julian understands that all of Christ's children birthed from him by nature shall be returned to him by grace.

ø

64

THE FIFTEENTH REVELATION

Julian had had a great desire to be delivered from this world; she was given to understand the sorrow on earth and the good in heaven. Even if there were no sorrow here, just the absence of the Lord was more than she could stand; she gained no pleasure in living from mere duty. Julian received an interior locution in which the Lord promised to give her comfort. She would be taken out of all her pain, sickness, and grief, and lifted up to heaven and filled with joy. Never again would she suffer. Why then should she not endure a while longer, since it was God's will and for his glory?

In this way, Julian was given to realize that God rewards us for our patience. By not knowing when the Lord will take us, no limit is set to our patience. At the same time, we should know that we are always at the point of being taken. All the pain we have on earth will be as nothing when we are lifted into bliss.

At this point in her revelations, Julian then had a bodily vision. She saw a fearsome, oppressive, shapeless body lying on the earth. Suddenly, it became a beautiful child, who quickly rose up into heaven. The wretchedness of our mortal flesh became the purity of our soul. She writes that it is more blessed for human beings to be taken away from pain than for pain to be taken away from us. If pain be taken away, it may return. So it is a greater comfort to know that we shall be taken away from pain. Such is our Lord's compassion. Then, in the revelation, God speaks to Julian and promises himself as her reward and that she will be filled with joy and bliss. It is God's will that we should often reflect upon this because it is greatly to God's glory.

When we fall back into ourselves and experience depression, spiritual blindness, and bodily pains on account of our frailty,

God wants us to know that he has not forgotten us. He promises us that we will never again have any kind of pain, sickness, or displeasure. It should not afflict us to persevere for a while since it is his will. God wants us to accept his commands and his consolations generously and to accept our own tarrying and sufferings lightly. When we accept them lightly, we give them less importance and the less pain they give us.

Ø

65

REVERENCE AND HUMILITY

The profundity of understanding Julian was given at the beginning of this chapter is as great as anything she has hitherto written. When someone freely chooses God in this life because of love, he or she can be positive that he or she is loved without end. Holding onto this on earth, we are as certain of the bliss of heaven as if we were already there. The more we delight in this certainty with reverence and humility, the more it pleases the Lord. Once again Julian affirms the foundational place of humility in the spiritual journey: we see God as wonderfully great, and ourselves as wonderfully small.

Reverence is a holy fear of our Lord. It is closely knit to humility. When these virtues are given to God's beloved, his presence can be seen and felt. This presence creates a wonderful security and a certain hope. God wants each of us to understand that his love is so great that individually we are united to him just as if everything he has done was done for us alone. This creates among us such a unity that no one can separate themselves from anybody else. Our soul is given to recognize that all the power of our enemy is held in God's hand and only God should we fear in love. All other fears are only a part of the pain and woe that is our lot in this life, which should be passed over as lightly as possible. All that God does shall be a great joy to us if we know him, love him, and reverently fear him.

Julian now reminds the reader that she has told of fifteen of her revelations given by God and has been renewed by further enlightening from the Holy Spirit. The first revelation began at about four in the morning and the others continued in a most beautiful and solemn order until three in the afternoon.

☙

66

A VISITOR

Julian is about to share her sixteenth revelation, which occurred the following night and was a confirmation of the first fifteen. But first, she reminds us of what happened at the beginning of her revelations. She was feeble and miserable, and her pain was suddenly taken from her for as long as the fifteen revelations were being shown. She was beginning to feel that she would live longer when her sickness returned. Once again, she felt as barren and dry as if her previous consolations were but a trifle and she grieved for the agony she felt and the lack of spiritual consolation. The reader will recall how flagrantly Julian is now ignoring the teachings of her visions, especially where she was told to accept her sufferings lightly.

At this point, she received a visit from a religious, possibly a Benedictine priest who staffed the parish, or possibly, even, he was a part of her sixteenth vision. Julian writes that the visitor laughed when she told him that she had been raving during the day, but he became very serious when she told him of her first vision, the bleeding face on the cross. This made her ashamed, because he took very seriously every word she said while she herself did not feel that she was taking it seriously. She had even referred to it as raving! Did she herself not believe the visions? She certainly did while she was having them and had intended to do so forever; now, like a fool, she let them pass from her mind. She realized how ungrateful she was to abandon God's revelations so imprudently. Graciously, God did not leave her to herself and, trusting in his mercy, she fell asleep.

(In some translations chapter 66 ends here and her dream of the devil begins a new chapter. In other accounts chapter 67 begins with the vision of her soul as a castle. We shall include the dream as part of chapter 67.)

∅

67

THE DREAM

What Julian describes in this chapter is not really one of her sixteen revelations, but only a realistic, sensual dream. It is something she knew and expected would happen. The devil would be given his opportunity to attack her before her death. There appeared before her a dreadful misshapen being who wanted to kill her but could not. She trusted that the Lord would protect her and he gave her the grace to wake up. She felt more dead than alive, and fled to the Lord and the faith of Holy Church. The people around her ministered to her until she was somewhat restored. She was brought to a peaceful rest, free from physical sickness or fear of conscience.

∅

68

THE SIXTEENTH REVELATION

(Note: some translations number the chapters one less than here: for instance, chapter 67 is included as part of chapter 66. These translations may have a total of 85 chapters rather than 86).

Julian's final revelation is of the deepest kind, shown to her spiritual eye and accompanied by interior locutions. In her heart, she sees her own soul as a glorious city, where sits the Lord Jesus, more noble than a bishop or king. He reigns in the soul gloriously and peacefully, whence he rules heaven and earth. His humanity sits at rest with his divinity. The soul is completely occupied with the Trinity, which rules and sustains all that exists solely by his might, wisdom, and goodness. The Blessed Trinity rejoices endlessly in the human soul, which it created as its eternal dwelling.

Julian is given to understand that our soul can never rest in anything beneath itself. The soul rejoices because God rejoices in the soul as the noblest of his works. The Trinity was pleased with the creation of the human soul, because it was made as fair and as precious as a creature could possibly be. Along with this, it is his will that our heart should be raised above all earthly things and all vain sorrows and rejoice in him.

ॐ

69

REASSURANCE IN TRUTH

This revelation was pleasing to Julian and she understood that the contemplation of these realities gave pleasure to God and great profit to us. This very contemplation made the soul like unto Him who is contemplated. She saw the Lord sitting and at rest and realized that this was a symbol of total security and endless dwelling. In the final revelation, the Lord assured Julian that it was indeed he who had granted her all these revelations. In words spoken only to her heart, the Lord told her these were no hallucinations, but that she was to accept, believe, and comfort herself in them.

It is a characteristic of interior locutions that they bring with them the unquestionable conviction of their own validity and truth. Julian recalls that in her first revelation the Lord told her that by his passion the fiend is overcome. In the same way in her final revelation, he tells her that she will not be overcome. All these teachings and all the comfort that comes from them are intended by God to be on behalf of all her fellow Christians.

The Lord makes known to Julian that she will not be overcome. This is done in a very powerful manner that she might feel comforted through any tribulations she may experience in the future. Julian stresses the fact that the Lord does not say that she will be free from trouble, bitter labor, or discomfort, but that they will not overcome her. Thus, in comfort and in tribulation, God wants us to realize that we should be strong in our trust. He loves us and delights in us and wills that we should love and delight in him, and all shall be well!

Ø

70

ANOTHER TEMPTATION

The devil returns to tempt Julian. This bears no similarity to her revelations, as the visitation is accompanied by a crass bodily vision with a vile stench and a dreadful, physical heat. It is also accompanied by muted whisperings, which she cannot understand but which are intended to foster despair. As is typical of such experiences, they superficially resemble a religious activity—in this case, the recitation of the Rosary, spoken with the mouth only and without any devout intention. Julian receives from the Lord the grace to trust in him and even to find comfort in spoken prayers just as she herself would comfort another person in such trials.

Julian sets her bodily eyes on the cross, and her tongue to speak of the Passion and the faith of Holy Church and her heart on God. In this way, Julian shows her fellow Christians that they have the same resources given to her to fight the temptations of the evil one, even if they have not personally experienced her revelations. They should use the same resources to keep themselves from sin.

This experience occupies Julian all that night until about six the following morning, by which time the temptations have passed but have left behind them their foul odor—perhaps as a kind of promise that they will return. Nevertheless, the fiend has been overcome by the passion of Christ, as the Lord had told her.

ℬ

71

STEADFAST FAITH

The Lord has given Julian no sign or token that her revelations were real, but only the assurance of his word in faith for her comfort and trust. Even when she abandons this by saying that her visions were ravings, the Lord mercifully reveals his revelation again within her soul with greater fullness, assuring her that these were not hallucinations, and that her faith would be her token of their truthfulness in the future. In this way, Julian will be able to keep his revelation, accept it, believe it, be comforted with it, trust in it, and never be overcome. Such faith will be in her heart until the end of her life so she can oppose blindness and spiritual enemies within and without.

Julian specifically speaks now to her fellow Christians who have not personally experienced such revelations. She tells them they will personally experience the faith that the Lord gives them to receive him and keep themselves in him. Unspoken, but obviously present here, is Julian's hope that her fellow Christians will accept and profit by her revelations. Nonetheless, in whatever way the Lord teaches them and in whatever way they perceive him, his goodness will allow their testing to strengthen them in faith.

The Lord's attitude toward our souls is glad and merry and he wants our souls to be gladly disposed toward him, so as to give him the reward he desires. We will manifest this disposition outwardly and the Lord will make it present inwardly. Therefore, we will be one with him and with each other.

The Lord sees us with three expressions. The first is that of his Passion. As we see it, this is sorrowful and grievous but still it is glad and joyful because he is God. The second is pity and compassion, which the Lord shows to us all, along with the protection of his mercy. The third is the blessed way in which the Lord will regard us for all eternity, so that when we are in pain and grief, he reveals his passion and helps us to bear it by his own power. In our time of sinning, he shows us compassion and protects us against our enemies. In this lifetime he mingles the third with these two expressions—that is, some part of his heavenly expression. This shows itself when, through grace, we receive illuminations of the Spirit granting us faith, hope, and love and every kind of sweet consolation.

ও

72

THE FACE OF GOD

The highest bliss that we can have is to possess God, truly seeing him, sweetly feeling him, and peacefully possessing him. God showed Julian part of this. The deepest pain we could possess, in opposition to this experience, comes from having anything to do with sin. The more grievous our sins, the deeper are we fallen from the vision of God. It can even seem to us as if we are in some part of hell because of our sorrow and pain. But truly, we are not dead in the sight of God, nor does he ever depart from us. Yet he will never have his full joy in us until we have our full joy in him. We are destined to this by nature and brought to it by grace.

For a short time, sin can seem deadly to us. Yet the more clearly the grace of loving shows to our soul the Lord's blessed face, the more we long to see it in its fullness. Our Lord is now dwelling in us, embracing us, and enclosing us, so he can never leave us. He is nearer to us than we can say or think. Still, we will continue to weep and seek and long for him until we see him clearly, face to face. Julian rejoices because our Lord is near to us and keeps us faithful; she grieves because we are so burdened with our mortal flesh and our sin that we cannot see his face clearly.

This weeping is sometimes physical, but it also has a more spiritual meaning. The natural attraction of our soul to God is so great that if he were to give us the most noble gifts ever created for our joy and comfort, we would still mourn and weep until we might see his blessed face. All the pain in the world would not bother us if we could see his face and every joy would be fulfilled. Three things we ought to know: we ought to know ourselves as we are by nature and by grace; we ought to know ourselves as regards our sin and our weakness (this is true humility); and we ought to know God (this is charity). Self-knowledge is foundational for knowledge of God.

✄

73

SLOTH AND FEAR

Julian begins this chapter by reviewing the three classical ways in which God reveals himself in private revelations. Bodily vision occurs when the Lord touches our imagination; locution occurs when the Lord speaks directly to the heart, although not necessarily with words but with a clear and unquestionable conviction; and finally, there is spiritual vision, the deepest form of revelation, and a sort of combination of the first two but on a deeper level, and which can only be communicated partially to others. Of Julian's sixteen revelations, many of them involved all three levels. She wishes here to speak more of the third level.

While God showed Julian sinfulness, in which all sin is understood, he emphasized two particular sins—sloth or impatience, and despair or spiritual fear. Christians who for the love of God hate sin and wish to dispose themselves to God's will, are most assailed by these. Therefore, he wants them to be known.

To help us, the Lord illustrates what patience he has in his Passion and also the joy that he has in it because of love. This is how gladly and easily we should bear our own pains. Only our ignorance of love prevents us from doing this. This is our greatest blindness. Some of us are aware that God is powerful and able to do everything, that he is all-wise and knows how to do everything, and that he is all-love and will do everything. But there we stop almost as if we do not believe this.

It is ignorance that most hinders us. We pay too much attention to ourselves and the sins we have done in the past, or even in the present. Thus, we fall into misery, which we mistake for humility but which is really a shameful blindness. We lack the certainty and the delight that the Lord wills we should have in his love. It is this love that makes the power and the wisdom of God be at our disposal so that we do not have unreasonable sorrow or doubtful fears about the forgiveness of our sins. We should forget our sins even as God forgets them.

∅

74

FOUR KINDS OF DREAD

There are four kinds of dread. The first dread comes from fear of being hurt. This can be useful for purging ourselves, such as through physical pain or sickness, which are not sinful but can be useful if they are borne patiently. The second dread is a fear of pain that comes from spiritual enemies and bodily death. It is present when we are asleep in sin and awakened by the gentle strength of the Holy Spirit. Thus we are moved to contrition and to seek the comfort and mercy of God. The third dread comes from doubt. The bitterness of doubt is turned into the sweetness of love by grace, because the Lord never wants us to doubt his goodness. The fourth dread comes from reverence. The only fear in us that pleases God is a gentle, reverent fear. It is in our nature to fear and to love: both are rooted in us by the goodness of God. It belongs to God's lordship to be feared reverently and it belongs to his goodness to be loved.

When we love, we fear, though we feel little of it. It is only a reverent fear that comes from God's grace. We can recognize it because it makes us flee from all that is not good and to fall into the Lord's arms, while at the same time recognizing our feebleness and his goodness. It is a fear that is gentle, gracious, good, and true. Anything other than this is wrong. The kind of fear we should have in this life is the same kind of fear we shall have in heaven. It comes from the graceful operation of the Holy Spirit and is gentle, courteous, and sweet. So we shall be close to God in love and courteous to God in fear. We should desire from our Lord that we love him meekly, fear him reverently, and trust him strongly. Without this no one can please God.

⌀

75

THREE NEEDS

We need three things. First of all, we need to love; then, we need pity in love for protection in a time of need; and, third, we need a longing in love to be drawn into heaven. God yearns for the whole of humankind; he yearns to teach us to know him and love him; he yearns to take us up into bliss; he yearns to fill us with this bliss forever. Pain and sorrow shall be ended and our bliss shall be increased because of it.

God has always prepared good things for us, hidden in himself until we are strong or worthy enough to receive them. Then he will reveal to us the reason for everything he has done and the reason for everything he has permitted. Our fulfillment will be so incredible that it will prompt in us so great a reverend fear that the very pillars of heaven shall quake and tremble. This kind of fear will be without pain; the trembling shall be from abundance of joy, marveling at God's greatness and our smallness. God is great and good. As it belongs to his goodness to be loved so it belongs to his greatness to be feared.

ℳ

76

THE LOVING SOUL AND SIN

Every soul the Lord showed to Julian was possessed of reverend fear. These souls, taught by the Holy Spirit, hate sin more because of its vileness than because of the pains of hell. Recognizing the kindness of the Lord, these souls hate sin rather than hell. God wants us to recognize sin and pray diligently and work hard so that we may not fall blindly into it, and if we do, that we may readily rise from it. We should flee from the thoughts of other humanity's sins as we flee from the pains of hell. These thoughts prevent us from seeing the fairness of God unless they prompt us to view these sins with sorrow and compassion and desire for God on the sinner's behalf.

The Lord showed Julian two opposites: the wisest thing and the most foolish she could do. The wisest thing is to do the will of Jesus, our friend, and never depart from him in well-being or in sorrow. The most foolish comes from our own folly and blindness and is the attitude that we take when we fall into sin ourselves. We assume a false dread of our own wretchedness, which makes us afraid to appear before the Lord. We forget him as a loving, loyal friend.

☙

77

LAUGHING GREATLY

Everything opposed to peace and love is from the devil. We may fall in our weakness but we can, through the grace of the Holy Spirit, rise to greater joy. If the devil gains anything from our falling, he loses much more in our rising, which is to him great sorrow and pain. The sorrow he would give to us is given back to him. Thus, the Lord scorns him. Julian is reminded here of the fifth revelation (chapter 13) where she laughed greatly at the devil's sorrow and made those around her laugh as well. Again, when she sees the Lord scorn the devil, she laughs greatly.

The remedy is to be humble, acknowledge our wretchedness, and flee to the Lord. The more humble we are, the more profitable it is for us. We know that we have deserved pains but our Lord is almighty and may punish us greatly; he is all wisdom and may punish us wisely, but he is all goodness, and loves us tenderly. It is a lovely humility in a sinful soul, through the grace of the Holy Spirit, when we are willing to accept the punishments our Lord himself wishes to give us. If we will remain content with him and all that he does, it will be very tender and even easy for us.

It was revealed to Julian that we ought meekly and patiently to bear the penance that God himself gives us, as we recall his blessed Passion. The penance we take upon ourselves by our own will was not revealed to her specifically; but when we recall the passion with pity and love, we suffer with the Lord, as did his friends who were present. Julian recalls here that, in the thirteenth revelation, the Lord does not want us to be immoderately depressed and impose penance on ourselves, but rather meekly to accept his will and all our life will be profitable penance.

Our life is a prison and a penance and God wants us to rejoice in the remedy—that is, he is with us, protecting us and leading us into joy. The way to heaven is heaven. We shall be comforted when we flee to the Lord. We shall be safe from every peril because our Lord wants us to be as familiar with him as heart may think or soul may desire. The Lord will teach us how to do this, for such is his delight and glory.

∅

78

KNOWLEDGE OF FOUR THINGS

Our sins are so horrible that the Lord shows them to us only by the gracious light of his mercy. He wants us to know four things: he is our very life and being; he protects us with his power and mercy when we are in our sin; he tells us when we are going astray and graciously protects us; he steadfastly waits for us because he wishes us to be united to him in love, as he is in us.

By this knowledge, we can see our sin to our own benefit. That shameful sight shall break down Pride and presumption. We must see that we are nothing but sin and misery. The Lord graciously adjusts this so that we can endure to see it as it is. Through contrition and grace, our Savior will heal us and unite us to himself. The Lord heals all humankind, the lowest and the highest (which is himself). He unites us together in love.

Julian says that she was so united to the Lord in love that she was unable to see her sin because of her joy. The Lord graced her to pay attention and taught her that it was necessary to have awareness of her sin and weakness along with her nobility. This was necessary for true humility, which, in turn, is necessary for salvation. This knowledge can come only from God. Yet again, Julian stresses that self-knowledge is foundational for knowledge and love of God.

ॐ

79

SIN IS INEVITABLE

In most of the chapters of her book, Julian is very much concerned to convey the message that sin is necessary and that God sees no blame or guilt in the sinner. It is because of sin that God is able to manifest his compassion, forgiveness, and love. In these later chapters, Julian seems to want to balance this idea, not by denying or contradicting it, but by making sure the reader understands the reality of sin, its vileness, the need for contrition and how it leads to humility.

With reflection and prayer, Julian's understanding of her revelations continues to grow and she is given a greater insight into their messages. She speaks now of a greater understanding of sin, both hers and those of her fellow Christians. Julian is given a comfort in this realization, a comfort large enough for her and for all Christians. She is taught to fear the uncertainty of her fidelity to the Lord because she does not know the measure of her sin. At the same time, the Lord assures her of his unchangeable love and that the souls of those who would be saved are never separated from that love. The fear she has been taught leads to humility, which saves her from presumption and gives her true comfort. This comfort is shown by a lovely lesson of our gracious Lord assuring her that anything opposed to this love is not from God. Our knowledge of God's plenteous love should never result in carelessness in guarding our hearts.

When we fall by frailty, our gracious Lord will touch us, call us, and preserve us. Then according to his will, we will see our misery and humbly acknowledge it. We will not, however, brood over it or be excessively miserable. We must give our attention to him, for he waits for us and is anxious that we be with him. We are his joy and delight; he is our salvation and our life.

ℬ

80

JESUS DOES EVERYTHING

Three things glorify God and help, preserve, and save us: the use of our natural reason; the common teaching of Holy Church; and the inward working of the Holy Spirit. God is the ground of our reason; God is the common teaching of the Church; and God is the Holy Spirit. These different gifts work in us all together for God and he wishes us to have great regard for them.

We have on earth a small basic knowledge of what we shall know in heaven. We know that God alone took our nature and Christ alone did the great works of our salvation: alone, he now dwells in us, rules us, and brings us to his bliss. The angels minister to us but Christ himself is nearest, and does not only everything that is necessary, but all that is full of honor for our eternal joy. He waits for us in sorrow and mourning because we are so united with him that everything in us that is beneficial is really Christ in us. Love never allows him to be without pity; though we are seldom aware of it, pity never passes from Christ until we are delivered from all our grief.

Christ is here for us and so it is proper to turn ourselves reverently and in haste to him. Whenever we are alienated from him by sin, we leave him to remain alone insofar as he is in us. We may act like this often, but in his goodness, Christ never leaves us alone. He is constantly with us, protecting and excusing us.

⌀

81

CHRIST IN OUR SOUL

The Lord reveals himself to us in many ways. On earth he has shown himself in his incarnation and his passion. Julian refers back to her third revelation in chapter 11, where she saw God in an instant of time. Here, he revealed himself as a pilgrim, journeying with us, and leading us to heaven. He also revealed himself several times, reigning as a lord in his own house (sixth revelation, chapter 14), and sitting enthroned at the right hand of God the Father (chapter 51). However, he reigns principally in the human soul, where he has a lasting city. Splendid is the place of his dwelling and he wants us to be more in touch with this, rejoicing in his steadfast love rather than sorrowing over our frequent sins.

The Lord sees our life here as a penance because of the substantial and natural desire we have for him, and which he has given us and helps us to bear. He glories in this kind of penance by which we live happily for love of him. This is what Julian means previously when she says that the penance the Lord gives is greater and more beneficial than any penance we impose upon ourselves. The Lord wants to see us longing with himself in his wisdom, truth, and justice. This is our loving penance that will accompany us to heaven. He wants us to set our hearts on this, not from the pain that we feel but for the bliss that we hope for.

⌀

82

WITH PITY, NOT WITH BLAME

The Lord explains the grief in our soul in this way: We do wish to live for his love gladly, suffering all the penance that may come to us. However, because we do not live without sin, we are depressed and sorry. It is his wish that we be not too much aggrieved by sin that comes to us against our will.

Julian sees that, because this life does not require us to live wholly without sin, the Lord looks on us, as he did on his servant in chapter 51, with pity and not with blame. We sin constantly but God loves us endlessly. He reveals the sin to us gently and we mourn prudently while turning ourselves to his mercy. We are nothing but sin, and he is nothing but goodness.

The sight of our sin makes us humble and allows us to know his everlasting love. Thus, we please him with our thanksgiving and praise and he holds us safely in his arms. The Lord desires that we should live with great longing for him and with great joy in him. This is true even though no one on earth is free from sin. Any other approach is not from God.

Julian is given to see that we are always protected by God's love whether we are in sin or in the process of being forgiven for our sin. In our own sight, we fall; in God's sight, we stand. In God's sight is the highest truth. In this life, it is good for us to realize both of these things at once. What God sees keeps us in spiritual comfort and joy; what we see keeps us in fear and humility.

&

83

FAITH IS OUR LIGHT

In the twelfth showing, the Lord told Julian "I Am He." This knowledge was somehow contained in every revelation and allowed Julian's spiritual senses to touch, see, and feel three properties of God: life, with a wonderful sense of familiarity; love, as a gentle graciousness; and light, as endless kindness. Julian experienced these properties coming from the goodness of God and her reason wished to be united to that goodness. Julian understood that reason is in God, is founded in human nature, and is the highest gift we have received from God.

Faith gives light to our reason. As light, it comes from our unending day—that is, our father, God; our mother, Christ; our lord, the Holy Spirit. We are given the light of faith in accordance with our need for it in the darkness of our night. This light causes our life, our pain, and our grief. However, because of this grief we earn eternal reward from God as, with mercy and grace, we believe in this light and walk in it wisely. When our grief is over, our eyes shall be opened and the light of our faith will be clearly seen as God: Creator, Savior, and Holy Spirit. Faith is our light in our night and that light is God.

☙

84

THE LIGHT IS ALSO LOVE

This light is love as well as faith. It also keeps us in hope. It is meted out for us by God's wisdom so that neither is it bright enough to see God clearly, nor does it completely bar him from us. It is the kind of light that allows us to work hard, thus earning

God's favor and reward. The Lord first gave Julian this understanding in the sixth revelation when he thanked her for her service and labor. Julian is given to understand that, in the end, everything shall be love. She has three understandings about love: love is uncreated, and this is God; love is created, and this is our soul in God; love is virtue, that is, a grace-filled gift of action by which we love God and all that God loves.

It is to be noted in these later chapters, after Julian explains her sixteenth and final revelation that she is giving us a kind of review or summary of all her showings. This is seen in her frequent references to particular earlier showings.

❧

85

ALL IS WELL

Despite our human folly and ignorance, the Lord looks upon us graciously and rejoices in us. We please him best by rejoicing in him. God has loved us and known us from without beginning. In this love he created us, protects us, and never allows us to be hurt in any way that might cause a lessening of our destined bliss. After Judgment Day in heaven, mysteries shall be revealed to us that are now hidden in God. Then we shall truly see that God ordained everything that has happened from all eternity. And it is well!

❧

86

NOT YET FINISHED

This book, begun by God's grace, is not finished. Let us join with God, who is the foundation of our praying, by accepting his grace to thank, trust, and rejoice in him. This book is not finished because the Lord wants its message to be known better than it is. We are his heavenly treasure, which he sees and loves even while we are here on earth. He wishes to increase our faith and comfort us in heavenly joy by drawing our hearts from our present darkness.

From the time her showings were first given, Julian desired to learn more of their meaning. Twenty years later, she was given an answer through spiritual understanding. Love was this answer. Love was how it was revealed. Love is what it means. She is to remain in this love that will never change. She will, however, know more and more of it.

Love is our Lord's meaning. Before he created us, he loved us. This love will never be taken away, and in it has been done everything that has been done. We had a beginning in creation but the love in which he made us was always in God. In this love, we have our beginning and we shall have it without end. And so ends the book of the revelations of the Lady Julian of Norwich, on whose soul may God have mercy.

(At the conclusion of this chapter, there is a colophon, an addition by a seventeenth century copier, presenting some sage advice to the reader):

> May this book come into the hands only of those who wish to be God's faithful lovers, who submit to the faith of Holy Church and who obey the holy teachings of men of virtuous life, settled age, and profound learning. Accept it in its

entirety and not simply those parts that are according to your pleasure. It is founded upon holy Scripture and Jesus will show this to all who humbly ask for his wisdom. Give him thanks for these showings that they may be a safe guide for you to everlasting joy.

Select Bibiography

Translations

Baker, Denice. *The Showings of Julian of Norwich*. New York: W. W. Norton, 2005.

Beer, Frances. *Julian of Norwich Revelations: Motherhood of God*. York University, Toronto: D. S. Brewer, 1998.

Colledge, Edmund and James Walsh. *Julian of Norwich Showings*. Mahwah, N.J.: Paulist Press, 1978.

John-Julian, Father. *A Lesson of Love: The Revelations of Julian of Norwich*. New York: Writers Club Press, 2003.

Del Mastro, M. L., *The Revelation of Divine Love in Sixteen Showings*. Liguori, Mo.: Liguori Press, 1994.

Skinner, John. *Revelation of Love: Julian of Norwich*, New York: Image Books, 1997.

Commentaries

Gatta, Julia. *Three Spiritual Directors For Our Time*. Cambridge, Mass.: Cowley Publications, 1986.

Llewelyn, Robert. *With Pity Not With Blame*. London: Darton, Longman and Todd, 1982.

Hide, Kerry. *Gifted Origins to Graced Fullfillment*. Collegeville, Minn.: Liturgical Press, 2001.

A mystic seeks conscious union
with God by contemplation +
self-surrender.

(P. 49) X Knowledge of self is
foundational to knowledge of
God . . .

CPSIA information can be obtained at www.ICGtesting.com
Printed in the USA
BVOW070142071111

275441BV00001B/1/P

9 781584 200888